THE ART
OF THE HOST

THE ART OF THE HOST

RECIPES AND RULES FOR FLAWLESS ENTERTAINING

―――――――――

ALEX HITZ

PHOTOGRAPHY BY IAIN BAGWELL

Rizzoli
NEW YORK

New York · Paris · London · Milan

FOR
AUNT LAURA
AND
MARY BOYLE HATAWAY

CONTENTS

We do not take a trip. A trip takes us.
—John Steinbeck

INTRODUCTION

In compiling the ideas, menus, and recipes for this book over the past six years—and looking through the more than two hundred fifty storage boxes of photographs, clippings, invitations, notes, and memorabilia from both sides of my family dating as far back as 1817—one of the main themes that can't be escaped, or underestimated, is the celebration of occasions. Somehow these scrapbooks, torn pages, yellowed photos, handwritten notes, and typed letters from my father's days as an air force photographer in Burma during the Second World War, with tales of his first taste of Darjeeling tea and digestive biscuits, seemed special, full of excitement and joy. Then, later, during his tenure at L'Institut d'Etudes Politiques in Paris, where even the crusty bread was rare and new. Not to mention the ethereal quality of time and place the missives from my mother to her mother contained about her heady first days of being a student at the Sorbonne in Paris, developing the same level of connoisseurship choosing a perfume on the Avenue Montaigne as trading dollars for francs on the black market, and being invited to the studios of Giacometti, and Picasso, to whom she was introduced by Alice B. Toklas.

Looking through these memories, my parents'—and their families'—lives seemed especially celebratory to me—and they knew it, as they kept absolutely every paper clip, rubber band, and staple—anything that would help someone to tell their story one day. These are the special souvenirs of uncommon lives well-lived, and after they'd been in storage for several years, I was delighted to spend six weeks with a crew of six people going through them all: categorizing them, wrapping them in acid-free paper, and just seeing them—some for the very first time.

Both sides gave parties—I have found Christening notices and menus from 1903, a program for a fiftieth anniversary party at Atlanta's Piedmont Driving Club for my great-grandparents in 1947, a box of unused invitations and the photo album for my grandparents' fiftieth anniversary, a black-tie dinner dance given by my father and his siblings in 1970. I found invitations to lunches and teas from the 1950s, copious wedding plans, diagrams, flowers

CLOCKWISE FROM TOP LEFT: *My grandmother with Mom and Aunt Laura, Cuba, 1948; my mother and grandmother boarding the* Queen Mary, *Southampton, 1957; Mom and Aunt Laura, Rome, 1961; Mom at the Palacio Real in Madrid, 1966; left to right: Mom, Cecilia Henry von Tupay, an unknown woman, and my grandmother, Rome, 1957.*

E HAUT
DE
CAGNES

"Le village
sur la
Colline
à deux
pas de
la Mer"

Photographed on board
R.M.S. QUEEN MARY

Linens on t
Shoes at De
Florence:

Venice: Sa

Rome: jewe
Ferr

Florence: Leo

Rome, Buso

specs, and menus from the 1960s. I found weekly menus for the cook from my grandmother's house in the 1940s, and pages and pages of listings of names of extra butlers and maids my parents brought in for big parties in the 1970s. More pages in a notebook entitled "Entertaining" with names, addresses, and phone numbers—complete with prefixes—of specialty caterers, bartenders, florists, and the like. I found my mother's guest lists, more than six hundred of them, starting in 1964 with her wedding to my father—fifty people at the wedding, one thousand at the reception—to the last lunch she gave in New York when my stepfather was conducting at Carnegie Hall, a week before she died in 1995.

What became abundantly clear was that Atlanta was a small town because both sides of my family appeared regularly, as often as weekly, in the "Rotogravure" of the *Atlanta Journal* and the *Atlanta Constitution*. But here's where it really got interesting to me: I found menus, guest lists for tables they hosted, place cards, and snapshots from trips to Europe aboard the the *Ile-de-France*, the *Queen Mary*, and the SS *France* dozens and dozens of times from 1947 to 1965, when the Jet Age was firmly established and the liners were finally retired. Time after time, these photos show my family preparing to see the world, hatboxes and evening dresses in hand. Travel is a Pandora's box, and the constant awakenings, curiosity, and overtones of my mother's sophistication came not from the sticking around the deb balls in Atlanta—but from, starting at a very early age, trotting the globe: to South America, Europe, Russia, and the near and Middle East, meeting the best and the brightest, and then bringing those experiences, those standards, and that style, to the house where I grew up in Atlanta, and to the parties given in that house.

"The Shaws do a considerable amount of entertaining," proclaimed a glowing valentine about my mother, "Caroline Shaw: Woman of the World," from the *Atlanta Constitution* in 1978. "Their parties are exciting," giddily proclaimed the author, "sometimes to groups of 250–300, although Mrs. Shaw's preference is for 8—so the guests can *really* talk to each other." As the wife of Robert Shaw, a thirty-six-time Grammy Award–winning symphonic conductor, and a Kennedy Center honoree, my mother's role was goodwill ambassador, chatelaine, hostess, confidante, and harlequin. She was brilliant at it, and not the least of her gifts was graciously hosting people at home for lunch or dinner. For charity, she raised millions of dollars doing so. And as a hostess, she and Robert crossed the racial and religious boundaries of the day, one cheese biscuit at a time. Her guests were the artistic luminaries of the 1970s and 1980s: Leontyne Price, Leonard Bernstein, Aaron Copeland, Marion Anderson, Beverly Sills, and Bobby Short—all of whom would come to perform as guest artists at the Atlanta Symphony. But these black or Jewish artists could not have lunch or dinner at the country club, so my mother served them impeccable Frenched-up Southern food at home, and became a noted hostess because of it.

Caroline came from a family where none of the women ever knew how to cook or wanted to. In Paris, and Tours, she lived with a grand family whose cook, Martine, had trained under Anthony Joseph Drexel Biddle, a peripatetic ambassador to a number of different European countries between the wars. Mom watched everything Martine did and took copious notes, many of which I found in those boxes I went through. The techniques and emphasis on ingredients—Martine's elegant foie gras soufflés, soubise, and lobster bisque—were a far cry from the hearty fare of my grandmother's cook, Sally, whose cornbread, fried chicken, and caramel cakes were surely delicious—but traditionally plain, probably under flavored for today's foodie palates, and introspectively Southern. When Mom was sent to the rue Christine to interview Alice B. Toklas for the school newspaper, in the apartment Alice had shared with Gertrude Stein for more than forty years—its walls covered in Picassos. Alice, by then a famous cookbook writer, gave her a lunch of a green herb salad with a mustard vinaigrette, crusty bread, and moussaka—a handwritten recipe that I found as a child in my mother's recipe box—and poire belle Hélène. For my mother, the DNA was sealed: simple hearty food bursting with flavor, every bite an occasion, and relaxedly but elegantly presented—not too much fuss. That DNA was passed to me not only by my mother—but also from other hostesses whom I have admired the most through the years, all over the world: Marguerite Littman in London; Brooke Hayward, Nan Kempner, Susan Gutfreund, and Louise Grunwald in New York; and Wendy Stark, Betsy Bloomingdale, and Connie Wald in Los Angeles.

When I was three years old, my mother married Robert, and life with them in the 1970s and 1980s was exciting. My own Pandora's box was opened. Robert guest-conducted the great orchestras of the world, and when he didn't we were traveling: to London and Paris first-class on Pan Am or TWA—I wish you could have seen what my mother wore on those planes—and later on the Concorde: that caviar! We went to Washington all the time, and often stayed at the White House, which, incidentally, was the first time I'd ever had blueberry corn cakes—leave it to the Carters to put grits in the pancakes. We spent our summers in Europe at our house in the Dordogne or exploring jet-set destinations: snorkeling and swimming at the brand-new Elounda Beach Hotel in Crete; hitting the links at Gleneagles in Scotland; waterskiing at Las Brisas in Acapulco; sunning and playing backgammon in Round Hill in Jamaica, touring the sites; and Scott's, Wilton's and The Veeraswamy from Claridge's in London; eating gravlax—my first-ever fish for breakfast—at The Grand Hotel in Stockholm, going again and again to have the gratin of spinach fettucine with ham at Harry's Bar just across from the Hotel Cipriani in Venice. And *always, always* France: My mother's first love. We went sailing and sea fishing from La Voile d'Or on La Côte d'Azur, and ate often at the Moulin de Mougins, a movie-star haunt. We had sauce Nantua with crevettes at one of my favorite fish restaurants ever, L'Oasis, in a Riviera town called La Napoule.

I've written so many times about L'Oustau de Baumanière in Provence and the tea with mint sorbet there, that I won't bore you again with that here, but suffice it to say, there is no substitute for exposure to quality, especially at such a young age, but at any age it's impossible to learn what's really good without it. In France, we set out to experience the finest dining of the day—la nouvelle cuisine—which I eventually came to loathe, as a nine- or ten-year-old child and early teenager. I only wanted the simpler brasserie food: poulet frites with béarnaise, or l'onglet with béarnaise, filet de saumon béarnaise, or anything else they served with béarnaise rather than nouvelle's layered, skimpy towers of something unidentifiable set on a plate. It's a philosophy I still have.

With the DNA set, after endless twists and turns, I embarked on a life in food. And now, everywhere I go to speak, or cook, or sign books, people line up to ask me what I would serve with what—or what is the best time of the year to serve this with

CLOCKWISE FROM TOP LEFT: *My mother (pregnant with me) introducing Alistair Cooke, Atlanta Historical Society, October 1968; my father's treasured medal from the maiden voyage of the SS France, 1962; my parents out on the town, May 1968; Mom and Robert Shaw on their wedding day, December 1973 (AP photo); with my father, Thanksgiving, 1972; my parents, April 1968.*

may 6th 1968.

Lv At
Lv Ke
Arr Z

A mor

Sun.
quart

A day

Lv Kl
quart
Hotel

Morni
train

A day
Night

Lv In
Golde

METROPOLITAN OPERA
TONIGHT 8:00 PM

Staff Photos—Joe McTyre

OPENING NIGHT AT THE FOX THEATER IS GALA
Mrs. Alex Hitz Jr., Junior League President, Mr. Hitz Attend

(AP)ATLANTA, Ga., Dec. 19--NEWLYWEDS--Robert Shaw, conductor of the
Atlanta Symphony Orchestra, and his bride, the former Mrs. Caroline
Sauls, pose following their marriage Wednesday in Atlanta. Before
coming to Atlanta in 1967, Shaw was associate conductor of the Clevela
orchestra. The couple will honeymoon in Florida. (AP WIREPHOTO)
(wam41715mbr/jnl) 1973

april 25th 1968

PRESIDENT DANCES WITH HUSBAND
Mr., Mrs. Alex Hitz Jr., at Junior League Ball

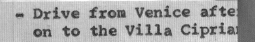

- Drive from Venice afte
  on to the Villa Cipria

- Drive from Asolo via V

- Drive from Verona to L
  Cernobbio on Lake Como

that. I thought I'd make it easy for you: a cookbook with recipes divided into perfect menus for every occasion. My hope is that you'll never again be at a loss as to what to serve when or how. The recipes are surely important, and these are painstakingly tested to ensure your success, but you'll need a few additional guidelines:

- Anything you do, must be done with style. A sure hand. Confidence.
- You must pay exquisite attention to detail. Don't leave anything to chance. Follow the French proverb: "A guest who has to ask for anything at the table is a host dishonored."
- Approach the planning of any event—whether it's a holiday or just another Tuesday—with a sense of occasion and joy. Make it look easy even if it's not.
- Always have an element of surprise—don't beat your party to death beforehand by telling all the details of the menu, guest list, and decorations—otherwise what is there to look forward to?
- Plan your parties with an appreciation of your guests and their gifts and talents in mind—and whom these talented and gifted people will sit next to . . .
- Never forget your party is your own piece of

theatre, and it exists in time. Don't ever bore the audience. First and foremost, parties are about people—so approach the planning of them with a sense of fun.

So, if you've never cooked for company but you want to, just start somewhere—a dessert, a salad dressing, an hors d'oeuvre. If you're more experienced, give a full menu a try: all of these are easily doable and spot-on. Never succumb to trends: great dining at home is based on the classics, and traditions that are handed down from family to family, place to place, culture to culture. If you make your parties about how much money you can spend, they will surely just be more expensive, not more fun or successful.

Finally, take what you've learned and make it your own. But if you can't, just make it mine, menus verbatim from the thirteen special ones here, plus the Essentials. Turn the lights down, and don't run out of wine. And, really, how bad can it be?

CLOCKWISE FROM TOP LEFT: *with Mom at her wedding to Robert, December 1973; with Robert at the Parthenon, summer 1975; with Robert in Jamaica, winter 1975; with President Carter at his 1977 inauguration; deep-sea fishing in the Cayman Islands, winter 1975; on the beach, Sea Island, Georgia, 1972.*

DATES AND PLACES
AFTER September 5th

5-10   Paris
11   Chartres, Mont St.
12   Tours

Restaurants:
La Tour d'Ar
Le Lapin Agi
Patachou - M
Le Chameleon
La Taverne d

THE THINGS I ALWAYS
AND ABSOLUTELY LOVE

NOTE: *I am not the person to call—nor, frankly, is this the book for you—if your predilections in dining indicate an affinity for drab gray walls, unstructured piccolo concertos, austere and oddly shaped tableware, "relevant" menus, deconstructed food, kombucha, quinoa, kale, or cold-pressed grapeseed oil, and I simply will not apologize for it.*

SILVER: Flatware or hollowware, ornate or plain—to me, more is always more, and never, ever, enough.

MONOGRAMMED LINENS: Mine or anyone else's—I am always so very happy to see them.

HEAVY CRYSTAL GOBLETS, DECANTERS, AND CHANDELIERS—and everything else William Yeoward makes.

CLASSIC COOKING WITH A TWIST: Again, no unrecognizable ingredients, no nitrous oxide, and certainly nothing from the science fair.

BIG, BOLD FLAVORS: Not the "little bit here" or a "little bit there" philosophy. Every bite should be an event, and a grand one, indeed.

BUTTER: This is self-explanatory and, certainly, no secret to fine cooks. Don't ever be afraid of it. And always use SALTED BUTTER. It's the secret to delicious food in France, where I learned it, and I do not care what the sneering purists say.

SALT: For these recipes, always use fine table salt. They are written for it, specifically, and will taste differently if you use other types or grains of salt.

ONIONS: If you only master the stages of cooking an onion, I'll bestow upon you a culinary Ph.D with summa cum laude honors.

GARLIC: Another inevitable truth is that it's impossible to have really good food without it. NOTE: *For these recipes, 1 clove makes about 1 teaspoon of minced garlic.*

CHEESE: Name one person who doesn't appreciate the pleasures of a gratineéd anything, whether they admit it or not. My favorite combination is Gruyère, Cheddar, Parmesan, and blue, all together—alone they're great but the combination is greater than the sum of its parts.

BRAISED MEATS: See the notes here about bold flavors and doing everything ahead of time.

DOING EVERYTHING AHEAD OF TIME: Not only is it easier, the flavors are always better. A true win-win.

TALL CANDLES: The ones I get are from the ecclesiastical supply house, and the higher they are, the closer they are to heaven.

VOTIVE CANDLES: There's no substitute for a bit of sparkle and warmth at every place.

ROSES FROM THE GARDEN, THE CORNER MARKET, OR THE POSHEST OF POSH FLORISTS: In a simple glass bowl, a silver beaker, or a zillion-dollar epergne, they never disappoint.

AND, OF COURSE, sumptuous, beautiful, and properly set tables filled with people I love.

ALWAYS

- Read a recipe thoroughly before you start to avoid any unwanted surprises. Many of these recipes say, "do at least 8 hours in advance, or, preferably, overnight," or "serve tomorrow," and that's not just a fancy: it's essential in order for them to develop their best flavors.

- Measure everything carefully if you want a consistently good result. "Eyeballing" leads to food that doesn't taste the same from one time to the next, and if someone loves one of your dishes that's the very last thing you want.

- Use salted butter and table salt for my recipes— they are written for it. I've already said this but I want to make sure you didn't miss it.

- Buy the best of whatever ingredient your recipe calls for—and plenty of it. Never skimp—whether it's frozen pizza, fried chicken, or truffles and caviar. If you're not feeling generous, cancel your party, but please do not parse out food. There should always be plenty of leftovers.

- Make a schedule for having a lunch or a dinner, and stick to it. Serve your lunches and dinners on time! Do not punish guests who have been punctual by waiting for, and thus rewarding, the bad-mannered ones who are late.

- Do everything ahead of time and heat it up. It tastes better, and is much less stressful, for you— and your guests. No one wants to see you freaking out and running around popping Xanax if your hasty sauté gets ruined!

- Set the table properly according to what your menu is: I know this sounds ridiculous but I can't tell you how many times I've seen hosts and hostesses serve, let's just say as an example, first courses of soups without soup spoons on the table. Conversely, if you aren't serving tea, I can guarantee you will not need a teaspoon.

- Keep all wines on the table, whether you have waiters to serve the wines or not, so that your guests can help themselves. There's nothing worse than waiting too long for a skimpy portion of wine from a waiter who's got too much else to do. The waiter can refill your glass, but do yourself—and your guests—a favor, and set the wines on the table.

- Consider where your guests will be seated, even if you don't have place cards. And remember, every single small detail for a party, regardless of how informal or grand the occasion, requires planning and forethought.

- Turn the lights down—no one came over to bear witness to a root canal or toe surgery.

- Make an effort—a huge effort, sweat all the small stuff—otherwise why are you having guests? No one has a gun to your head to entertain, so if you do it, be all-in, or not at all; and do everything *before* your guests arrive so they don't see you sweat. Nothing can ruin a party quicker than watching the host straining to get the job done. Parties are worth the extra effort, but they must look seamless, and simple, though they never, ever are.

- Have candles and flowers. I always have candles at special holiday lunches even though Emily Post says no candles during the day . . . There's so much else to offend our sensibilities now, that I think perhaps, dear Emily, we can let that one go.

- Remember that anything can go wrong, and often does. Nothing's perfect. But a party will be successful, regardless, if you keep smiling—and have plenty of wine.

NEVER

- Stop smiling. I realize I've said this before but at parties, just about anything can go wrong, and often does, things far out of your control. Never stop smiling, and every little disaster will be A-OK.

- Use your guests as guinea pigs. Be 100 percent sure of everything you'll serve beforehand. They deserve the best you have to offer.

- Plan menus that are trendy or too complicated because, as Karl Lagerfeld put it best, "The last step after trendy is tacky."

- Ask if your guests have any food allergies. I have my own, and oftentimes cannot eat what is served to me. I manage always, thrilled to be included at the table—not ever concerned that this could be my last meal on earth—and I simply do not want to discuss my allergies with my hosts or waiters. Somehow this practice of asking has become acceptable, but it's *really* not.

- Have a cocktail "hour" that is any longer than forty-five minutes.

- Make the music too loud. It sets people on edge, and can even make them leave. This is lunch or dinner, and not a rock concert.

- Let your guests see you sweat. This is underscored in the "Always" section, but I really cannot ever say this enough.

- Lose control of your table. If you see your guests on their cell phones, remember they took the first rude steps so it's 100 percent acceptable to say, "Please no phones. I enjoy your company." Mark my words: there has never, ever been a party made better by having its guests working their phones. Be strong and do not succumb to the tyranny of this mounting addiction, 'cause let's face it: those just aren't that much fun at parties. This will not be the last time you hear this from me.

- Try to please everyone. Be a considerate, generous host, with good intentions when you plan your menus and parties. But never forget that the more people you try to please by accommodating their special diets or eating habits, the more times you will fail. Every effort should be your best; simple, impeccable, delicious, hearty food, candlelight and plenty of wine will ensure you succeed—but giving your guests too many choices to suit them personally is the sign of a very insecure host. Your dining room is not a short-order kitchen. By making a generous and thoughtful effort, even if not everyone likes or can eat everything, your party will be more than good enough, a great success—a triumph, even—and if it's not, please get some new friends.

> *The bitterness of poor quality remains*
> *long after the sweetness of low price is forgotten.*
> —Benjamin Franklin

WHAT TO HAVE

- 12 place settings of the best sterling silver flatware you can afford—and use it every single day. Every day! Do not only use it for special occasions, as lifetimes go by and, if you're not in the habit, you may forget to use it. Remember, every day is a special occasion.

- 12 matching plates for three courses: first course, dinner, dessert. The patterns can vary from course to course, but not from place to place.

- 12 really good linen dinner napkins, preferably with monograms on them. They can be handed down from generation to generation. Even if your table can only seat 4, 6, or 8, chances are you could feasibly have more guests for a buffet sometime. My favorite number for plates, glasses, and linen napkins is 12.

- At least 12 linen cocktail napkins, preferably monogrammed.

- 12 crystal water goblets. Or silver. You can't go wrong either way.

- 12 all-purpose wine glasses—I think the best bang for the buck is Riedel.

- Candlesticks and votive candles—any questions, please see "Always," page 18

- A large KitchenAid stand mixer, the largest and costliest one you can afford. I say large here for a reason: the large size can do smaller quantities, but the other-way-round doesn't work. You'll have it forever.

- A large Cuisinart food processor, for the same reason as the stand mixer

- A small Cuisinart food processor

- An immersion blender

- Pyrex 9 by 13-inch glass baking dishes—get at least 6

- At least 5 heavy metal baking sheets

- A set of various-sized stackable metal mixing bowls

- Rubber spatulas—I can never have enough of these

- White cotton aprons and kitchen towels that are usable and not too expensive or fancy as they get ruined so quickly

- Heavy metal measuring spoons

- A really good set of biscuit cutters

- Liquid measuring cups

- Dry measuring cups

- A kitchen scale

- 3 sizes of ladles and 3 sizes of scoops

- A couple of Le Creuset Dutch ovens

- A set of various-sized porcelain ramekins for making soufflés or reheating dishes and serving them at the table

RIGHT: *For splendid glassware like this, go see Nick Brock Antiques in Dallas.*

> *I don't like 'this' cooking or 'that' cooking . . . I like good cooking.*
> —James Beard

THE ESSENTIALS

PERFECT-EVERY-TIME PÂTE BRISÉE

ESSENTIAL DILL VINAIGRETTE

THE EASIEST, BEST VINAIGRETTE
IN THE WORLD

PERFECT HOMEMADE MAYONNAISE

BEL-AIR ONION PUFFS

LUSCIOUS CARROT AND
GINGER SOUP

MINI GRILLED CHEDDAR AND
GOAT CHEESE SANDWICHES

PERFECT VICHYSSOISE

BUTTER LETTUCE SALAD
WITH CHIVES AND HERBS

EASY TOMATO AND PESTO TART

GRUYÈRE AND BLUE CHEESE TART
WITH CARAMELIZED ONIONS

PERFECT POACHED SALMON
WITH GREEN HERB SAUCE

CURRIED CHICKEN SALAD
WITH GOLDEN RAISINS

HARRY'S GRAVLAX WITH
"GRAVLAX SAUCE"

CHICKEN CHILI WITH WILD
MUSHROOMS AND CORN STICKS

CHICKEN, VEAL, OR SHIRT
CARDBOARD PICCATA

PERFECT CORN STICKS OR
CORNBREAD

TAGINE OF LAMB WITH APRICOTS
AND ALMONDS

TO-DIE-FOR ALE-BRAISED BRISKET

PERFECT CREAMED SPINACH

ROSEMARY ROASTED POTATOES

BROCCOLI AND CHEDDAR GRATIN

EASY OVEN-BAKED POTATO CHIPS

RISOTTO ALLA MILANESE

FOOLPROOF BOURBON
PECAN PRALINES

BOURBON WHIPPED CREAM

"DEVOTEDLY, BETTY'S"
TIPSY AMBROSIA

CONNIE'S CHOCOLATE SAUCE

GRAND MARNIER SOUFFLÉ WITH
VANILLA GRAND MARNIER SAUCE

These recipes, the only ones in the book not divided into specific menus, are abiding favorites of mine—and my guests—and are easy, impressive, and doable by all manner of unskilled and skilled cooks and hosts, veteran or newbie alike. Pay attention, read, cook, and serve, and, *abracadabra*, success! No more being overwhelmed by the thought of cooking and serving guests at home. We won't call it entertaining because that's a big word I try rarely to use.

This chapter is your secret weapon—the splendid recipes always to have up your sleeve in case you're ever at a loss, proverbial aces in the hole for hosting people at home for breakfast, lunch, or dinner. A mere walk through these pages and you can cook—and serve these dishes proudly to anyone. Even if you begin by just making a pie crust, a salad dressing, or an hors d'oeuvre, it's a good start, and you're on the road to never being overwhelmed or daunted by the thought of hosting people and cooking for them. If you're just a beginner or you're uneasy in your culinary skin—or you've failed before and succumbed to the jeers of taunting family members or smug friends—make one of these recipes, and then you've done it. And if you can only do one thing, already that's something, and one more thing than you did before. Do it again, and all of a sudden you've mastered a dish, and you're on your way to being a fabulous cook—take all the credit: I'll keep your secret.

RIGHT: *EVERYTHING tastes better on Herend china.*

Perfect-Every-Time Pâte Brisée

Makes 1 crust, enough for a 9 by 13-inch baking pan

2 cups all-purpose flour
½ teaspoon salt
½ teaspoon sugar
8 tablespoons (1 stick) cold butter, cut into quarters
3 tablespoons butter, melted
5 tablespoons ice water

In the bowl of a food processor fitted with a metal blade, pulse all the ingredients until coarse crumbs form. Do not over-process the crumbs or the crust will be tough. Pour the crumbs out onto a floured surface and knead them a couple of times to bring them together into a dough. Be careful not to over-knead the dough or, again, the crust will be tough. Roll the dough into a ball and cover it tightly with plastic wrap. Set the dough in the refrigerator and let it rest for at least 1 hour—or it can be kept in the freezer for up to six months before defrosting and rolling it out.

Preheat the oven to 375°F, and butter a 9 by 13-inch metal baking pan. Remove the dough from the refrigerator and set it on a floured surface. Roll it out to a ¼-inch thickness and place it in the prepared baking pan, pressing it against the sides and the bottom so that there is no air between the pan and dough. Prick the dough all over with a fork to get rid of any air bubbles and to ensure it doesn't buckle when cooking. Place the pan in the oven and let the dough bake for 15 to 18 minutes, until it is golden brown. Let the crust cool completely before filling.

Essential Dill Vinaigrette

Makes 4 cups

1 cup red wine vinegar
3 tablespoons minced garlic
2 tablespoons dry mustard
2 tablespoons dried dill
1 tablespoon salt
1 teaspoon ground black pepper
3 cups tasteless vegetable oil, see Note

In a medium bowl, combine the vinegar, garlic, mustard, dill, salt, and black pepper. Whisk them together to blend them thoroughly. Add the oil slowly, whisking vigorously and constantly to make an emulsion. Refrigerate the vinaigrette in an airtight container for up to 1 week. Whisk the vinaigrette before serving if it has separated.

Note: For vinaigrettes, I almost always use plain, tasteless vegetable oil. There are many varieties, so use the one you like best, but it's worth mentioning that whenever I try canola oil for dressings, I always throw the finished product out. For me, it's too strongly flavored. Same thing with olive oil—with the exception of the next recipe. As for the tasteless oil, I use Wesson, similar to one I had in France as a child. Big secret: the vinaigrettes in France are always made with tasteless oil; olive oil is reserved only for times when you really want that strong flavor.

Those round pie plates are such a lot of trouble to me. Just make all your pies, quiches, and tarts in metal baking pans like this, and cut them however you like—sooooo much easier!

The Easiest, Best Vinaigrette in the World

Makes ¾ cup

¼ cup freshly squeezed lemon juice
2 tablespoons minced shallot
2 tablespoons Dijon mustard
¼ teaspoon salt
⅛ teaspoon ground black pepper
6 tablespoons olive oil

Whisk the lemon juice, shallots, mustard, salt, and pepper together in a small bowl to make an emulsion. Slowly drizzle in the oil while whisking, or this can also be done in a food processor if you want to make it even easier.

Perfect Homemade Mayonnaise

Makes 1 cup

3 egg yolks
4 tablespoons freshly squeezed lemon juice
1¼ teaspoons Dijon mustard
¼ teaspoon dry mustard
¾ teaspoon salt
⅛ teaspoon ground black pepper
¾ cup tasteless vegetable oil

In the bowl of a food processor fitted with the metal blade, combine the egg yolks, lemon juice, Dijon mustard, dry mustard, salt, and black pepper and process them until they are thick and frothy, approximately 2 minutes. Slowly pour the oil through the feed tube, and turn the machine off when you have finished adding the oil. *Note:* My mayonnaise is much looser and more liquid than store-bought, so just know that when you see the more liquid sauce-like consistency you have succeeded not failed!

Bel-Air Onion Puffs

Makes 15 to 20 small hors d'oeuvres

4 tablespoons (½ stick) butter
3 slices good-quality white sandwich bread, such as Pepperidge Farm
¼ cup Perfect Homemade Mayonnaise, recipe opposite, or Hellman's
¼ cup grated Parmesan cheese
3 green onions, both green and white parts, minced
⅛ teaspoon salt
¼ teaspoon cracked black pepper

Preheat the oven to 350°F. Line a heavy baking sheet with parchment paper.

Melt the butter in a small heavy saucepan over medium-high heat. Assemble the pieces of bread on the prepared baking sheet and, using a pastry brush, paint both sides with the melted butter. Place the buttered bread in the oven and bake it for 12 minutes.

Remove the baking sheet from the oven, turn the bread, and place it back in the oven for another 12 minutes, until the toasts are fully cooked through. Remove them from the oven and let them cool for at least 20 minutes—or store in an air-tight container for up to 3 days.

Preheat the oven to broil. In a small bowl, combine the mayonnaise, Parmesan cheese, green onions, salt, and pepper. Spread the mayonnaise and cheese mixture evenly over the three slices of toast, place them on a parchment-lined baking sheet, and broil them in the oven for 4 to 5 minutes, until they are bubbling and golden brown. Remove them from the oven. Cut the puffs with a 1-inch biscuit cutter and serve them immediately, or set them aside and let them cool for up to 2 hours before reheating them in a low oven and serving them warm.

Luscious Carrot and Ginger Soup

Makes 2½ quarts, enough for 8 to 10 servings

2 tablespoons butter
4 pounds carrots, peeled and sliced
2 tablespoons grated fresh ginger
4 cups chicken stock
2 teaspoons salt
½ teaspoon ground white pepper
1 cup heavy cream

Melt the butter in a Dutch oven or large heavy stockpot over medium heat. When the foaming has subsided, add the carrots and ginger, and sauté them for about 5 minutes, until they start to release their liquid. Add the chicken stock, and increase the heat, bringing the mixture to a boil. Reduce the heat, cover the pot, and let the carrots simmer until they are tender, 15 to 20 minutes.

Let the mixture cool for 10 minutes. Transfer the mixture in batches to a food processor fitted with a metal blade, and puree it until it's completely smooth. Return the mixture to a clean pot. Add the salt, pepper, and cream and fully heat the soup through, bringing it to a bubble but not a boil. Serve the soup immediately or let it cool, cover it, and refrigerate it for up to 3 days before reheating it to serve it later.

Mini Grilled Cheddar and Goat Cheese Sandwiches

Makes 18 small hors d'oeuvres

4 ounces white Cheddar cheese, grated
2 ounces goat cheese
4 slices good-quality white sandwich bread,
    such as Pepperidge Farm
4 tablespoons (½ stick) butter

In a small bowl, blend the cheeses together with a wooden spoon until they are well combined. Place the pieces of bread on a counter, and put half of the cheese mixture on two of the pieces of bread. Top the cheese-covered bread with the remaining slices of bread. Press down on the top layer of bread so the cheese mixture covers the bread to its edges.

In a large heavy skillet over medium-low heat, melt 2 tablespoons of the butter. When the foaming has subsided, sear the sandwiches on one side until they are lightly golden brown. Remove the sandwiches from the pan. Add the remaining 2 tablespoons butter, put the sandwiches back in the skillet, uncooked side down, and cook them until they are seared to the same doneness and color.

Remove the seared sandwiches from the heat and let them cool fully. Trim off the crusts, and cut them into 9 small squares. Reheat them at 300°F on a parchment-lined baking sheet when you're ready to serve.

Perfect Vichyssoise

Makes 8 cups, enough for 8 to 10 servings

4 tablespoons (½ stick) butter
8 leeks, the white parts only, washed and thinly sliced
1½ pounds medium-size Russet potatoes, peeled and cut into small cubes, then set aside in water to prevent browning
3 cups chicken stock
2 cups milk
1 cup heavy cream
¼ teaspoon ground nutmeg
2 teaspoons salt
½ teaspoon ground white pepper
4 fresh chives, finely chopped, for garnish

Melt the butter in a large heavy stockpot over medium-low heat. When the foaming has subsided, add the leeks and sweat them, carefully, for 5 to 7 minutes, until they are just translucent, making sure they do not brown at all. Add the potatoes, and stir the mixture to thoroughly combine. Add the chicken stock, and bring the mixture to a boil. Reduce the heat to low and let the soup simmer, uncovered, for approximately 35 minutes, until the leeks and potatoes are very soft.

Remove the stockpot from the heat and allow the soup to cool for a few minutes. Puree the soup slowly, and in small batches, in a food processor, or all at once with an immersion blender, until it is completely smooth. Return the soup to the stockpot, and add the milk, cream, nutmeg, salt, and white pepper. Return the soup to a boil, and then reduce the heat and let it simmer for another 5 minutes. Let the soup cool completely then cover it and refrigerate for at least 8 hours before serving it cold. You can make the soup up to 3 days ahead. Garnish individual servings with the chopped chives.

Butter Lettuce Salad with Chives and Herbs

Makes 6 to 8 servings

2 heads Bibb lettuce, torn
2 heads butter lettuce, torn
½ cup chopped fresh chives
¼ cup chopped fresh tarragon or dill
¼ cup chopped fresh flat-leaf parsley
The Easiest, Best Vinaigrette in the World, page 28
Salt and freshly-ground black pepper

Combine all ingredients in a large bowl, being extra-generous with the dressing. Toss the salad at least forty times, and serve. Don't be afraid to do this ahead of time even if you're worried about the lettuces getting soggy—that's just exactly the way I like them.

Easy Tomato and Pesto Tart

Makes 8 to 10 servings

Perfect-Every-Time Pâte Brisée, page 27, cooled

FOR THE PESTO:
1½ cups very firmly packed basil, leaves only
1 cup toasted almonds
12 cloves garlic, peeled
½ cup grated Parmesan cheese
¾ teaspoon salt
¼ teaspoon ground black pepper
½ cup olive oil

FOR THE TOMATOES:
3–4 small tomatoes, very thinly sliced, to make 18 slices
½ teaspoon salt, divided
¼ teaspoon ground black pepper, divided
1 tablespoon grated Parmesan cheese

Preheat the oven to 350°F.

TO MAKE THE PESTO:
Combine the basil, almonds, garlic, Parmesan, salt, and pepper in the bowl of a food processor fitted with the metal blade. Process them until they are smooth, then slowly add the olive oil through the feed tube while you're still letting the processor run.

TO ASSEMBLE THE TART:
Place the tomatoes on a rack so that they can drain, and season them with ¼ teaspoon of the salt, and ⅛ teaspoon of the ground black pepper; turn them over and season the tomatoes with the remaining salt and pepper. Place 6 tomato slices on the bottom of the crust and then spread the pesto evenly over them. Lay the remaining 12 slices of tomato on top of the pesto layer, arranging them neatly, slightly overlapping them if need be. Sprinkle the tomatoes with the cheese before baking the tart for 30 minutes. Serve the tart warm, room temperature, or cold.

Gruyère and Blue Cheese Tart with Caramelized Onions

Makes 8 to 10 servings

Perfect-Every-Time Pâte Brisée, page 27, cooled
3 tablespoons butter
2 medium yellow or white onions, peeled, and diced
¼ cup golden sherry, divided
1 cup grated Gruyère cheese, firmly packed
1 cup crumbled blue cheese, firmly packed
4 eggs, slightly beaten
1½ cups heavy cream
1 tablespoon freshly squeezed lemon juice
¼ teaspoon salt
¼ teaspoon cracked black pepper
½ teaspoon dried thyme
½ teaspoon ground nutmeg

Preheat the oven to 350°F.

Melt the butter in a large heavy skillet over medium-high heat. Once the foaming has subsided, add the onions and cook them until they are translucent and starting to brown, approximately 15 minutes. Turn up the heat, and let the onions fully brown, another 10 minutes or so. Add 2 tablespoons of the sherry after 8 minutes of the cooking time has elapsed. Remove the onions from the heat, and let them cool slightly.

In a medium bowl, combine the Gruyère, blue cheese, eggs, cream, lemon juice, salt, cracked black pepper, thyme, nutmeg, the remaining 2 tablespoons sherry, and the onions. Using a rubber spatula or wooden spoon, spread the mixture evenly over the pâte brisée. Bake the tart for 35 to 40 minutes, until it's golden brown. Remove the tart from the oven and let it cool for at least 20 minutes before slicing. It can be served warm, room temperature, or cold.

Perfect Poached Salmon with Green Herb Sauce

Makes 6 to 8 servings

2 tablespoons minced shallots, divided
1 (2 pound) skinless salmon fillet, deboned
½ teaspoon salt, divided
¼ teaspoon ground black pepper, divided
1½ cups white wine
2 tablespoons butter, cut into quarters
Green Herb Sauce, recipe follows

Preheat the oven to 375°F.

Add 1 tablespoon of the minced shallots to a 9 by 13-inch baking dish, spreading them evenly on the bottom. Place the salmon in the baking dish and season with ¼ teaspoon of the salt and ⅛ teaspoon of the pepper before turning it to season it with the remaining salt and pepper. Add the remaining tablespoon of shallots on top of the salmon, spreading them evenly. Pour the white wine over the salmon and then dot the salmon with the butter. Cover the salmon with a sheet of wax paper, pressing it down onto the salmon. Place the salmon in the oven, and bake it for 10 to 12 minutes, until it's just cooked through. Remove the salmon from the oven, and set it on a plate to cool; discard the liquid. Once it's cool, cover the salmon with plastic wrap, and refrigerate it for at least 3 hours, and up to 3 days. Serve the salmon cold with the Green Herb Sauce.

GREEN HERB SAUCE
Makes 1½ cups

Perfect Homemade Mayonnaise, page 28, or Hellman's
1 tablespoon minced garlic
1 bunch flat-leaf parsley
1 bunch watercress
4 sprigs tarragon
4 sprigs mint
10 sprigs basil
2 tablespoons freshly squeezed lemon juice
½ teaspoon salt
¼ teaspoon ground black pepper

In the bowl of a food processer fitted with the metal blade, combine all of the ingredients and process them until they are completely smooth. Transfer the sauce to a bowl and cover it with plastic wrap. Refrigerate the sauce for at least 6 hours, but preferably overnight, to allow the flavors the chance to get to know each other.

Curried Chicken Salad with Golden Raisins

Makes 12 to 15 servings

2 tablespoons butter
2 pounds skinless chicken breasts or thighs
1½ teaspoons salt, divided
¼ teaspoon ground black pepper, divided
1½ cups Perfect Homemde Mayonnaise, page 28,
    or Hellman's
½ cup dry white wine
½ cup Major Grey's chutney
4 tablespoons curry powder
1½ cups diced celery
1½ cups chopped green onions, both green and
    white parts
¾ cup golden raisins
¾ cup dark raisins
¾ teaspoon cracked black pepper

Melt the butter in a large heavy skillet over medium heat. Season the chicken with ¼ teaspoon of the salt and ⅛ teaspoon ground black pepper per side. When the foaming in the pan has subsided, add the chicken, and sear it until it is brown on the outside, approximately 3 minutes per side. Sear the chicken for another 3 to 5 minutes per side, until it is fully cooked through but still very moist. Remove the chicken from the pan, and let it cool for at least 15 minutes before shredding it with your hands.

In a large bowl, combine the shredded chicken with the mayonnaise, white wine, chutney, curry powder, celery, green onions, golden and dark raisins, the remaining 1¼ teaspoons salt, and the cracked black pepper. Refrigerate the salad, covered, for at least 8 hours, but preferably overnight, to allow the flavors to blend well. Serve the salad cold.

Harry's Gravlax with "Gravlax" Sauce

Harry was Mary Boyle Hataway's husband and his gravlax, my absolute favorite.

Makes 24 to 32 servings

¼ cup sugar
2 tablespoons plus 2 teaspoons salt
¾ teaspoon ground white pepper
¾ teaspoon ground allspice
2 ounces fresh dill, about 42 sprigs
1 (2 pound) salmon fillet, skin-on and deboned
"Gravlax Sauce," recipe follows

In a small bowl combine the sugar, salt, white pepper, and allspice and whisk them together.

Place the salmon in a 9 by 13-inch baking dish skin side down. Coat the salmon with the sugar-spice mixture and gently press it into the salmon skin. Turn the salmon over, and coat the other side with the mixture. Transfer the salmon to a plate. Spread out the mixture that remains in the dish and evenly spread the dill sprigs on top. Lay the salmon on top of the dill, skin side down. Cover the salmon with plastic wrap, making sure it touches all visible surfaces of the salmon. Cover the dish with another layer of plastic wrap, and refrigerate the salmon for 3 days to cure it.

Slice the gravlax to the desired thickness—I prefer about ¼ inch—and serve it with the sauce alongside.

Note: Gravlax freezes so well, why not keep it on hand for up to 3 months to slice for that whatever, whenever?

"GRAVLAX" SAUCE
Makes 2½ cups

1½ cups Perfect Homemade Mayonnaise, page 28, or Hellman's
1 cup sour cream
1½ teaspoons freshly squeezed lemon juice
1⅛ teaspoons salt
3 tablespoons Dijon mustard

Stir the ingredients together in a small bowl until they are thoroughly combined.

RIGHT: *How easy are these if you've already got Harry's Gravlax on hand?*

Chicken Chili with Wild Mushrooms and Corn Sticks

Makes 20 to 24 servings

3 pounds boneless, skinless chicken breasts
5¼ teaspoons plus ⅛ teaspoon salt, divided
¾ teaspoon ground black pepper, divided
9 tablespoons (1 stick plus 1 tablespoon) butter
4 cups diced onions
2 tablespoons minced garlic
2 red peppers, cored, seeded, and diced
2 yellow peppers, cored, seeded, and diced
1 pound shiitake mushrooms, sliced
2 (28-ounce) cans whole peeled tomatoes in juice
1½ cups chicken stock
1 teaspoon chili powder
1⅛ teaspoons ground cumin, divided
¼ teaspoon cayenne pepper
1 teaspoon dried thyme
¼ teaspoon cracked black pepper
1½ teaspoons freshly squeezed lemon juice
3 tablespoons balsamic vinegar
2 tablespoons dark brown sugar
Perfect Corn Sticks or Cornbread, page 44
Sour cream, shredded cheddar, and chopped green
    onions, for garnish

Combine the chicken breasts, 1½ teaspoons of the salt, and the ground pepper in a medium bowl. Toss the chicken breasts thoroughly, until no seasonings remain in the bowl. Melt 3 tablespoons of the butter in a large heavy skillet or Dutch oven over medium-high heat. When the foaming has subsided, add the chicken breasts, and brown the first side, approximately 3 minutes. Turn the chicken, and brown the other side, approximately 2 minutes. Transfer the chicken to a cutting board (it will not be cooked through), and cut it into large chunks. Place the chicken in the bowl of a food processor fitted with a metal blade, and process it until the chicken is shredded. Set the chicken aside.

Melt an additional 2 tablespoons of the butter in the same heavy skillet over medium-high heat. Add the onions and garlic, and cook them until the onions are translucent, about 3 minutes. Remove the skillet from the heat. Melt another 4 tablespoons of the butter in a large heavy stockpot or Dutch oven over medium-high heat. When the foaming has subsided, add the red and yellow peppers, the shiitake mushrooms, the tomatoes and their juice, chicken stock, chili powder, 1 teaspoon of the cumin, and the cayenne pepper. Stir them to combine well. Add the sautéed onions and garlic, and the shredded chicken. Let the chili simmer over a medium-high heat, uncovered, for 20 minutes, stirring occasionally. Reduce the heat to medium and simmer for an additional 20 minutes.

Add the remaining salt and cumin, and then the thyme, cracked black pepper, lemon juice, balsamic vinegar, and the dark brown sugar. Bring the chili to a boil again, and let it boil for an additional 20 minutes, until the chili has thickened and the liquid has reduced by about one-quarter. Let the chili cool in the pot, then cover it, and refrigerate it overnight. Serve the chili garnished with sour cream, shredded cheddar, and green onions with Perfect Corn Sticks or Cornbread alongside.

Chicken, Veal, Turkey, or Shirt Cardboard Piccata

Makes 6 servings

2 pounds boneless, skinless chicken breasts, veal scallopini, or turkey cutlets, sliced horizontally, then cut in half again
1½ teaspoons salt, divided
¾ teaspoon ground black pepper, divided
8 tablespoons (1 stick) cold butter, divided
2 tablespoons olive oil
2 large shallots, chopped
1 teaspoon minced garlic
1 cup dry white wine
¼ cup freshly squeezed lemon juice
1 cup chicken stock
2 tablespoons chopped flat-leaf parsley
2 lemons, one sliced thinly and one cut into wedges, for garnish

Place the pieces of chicken between two layers of plastic wrap. Using a meat tenderizer or cleaver, pound the chicken pieces to a ¼-inch thickness. In a large bowl, combine the chicken, 1 teaspoon of the salt, and ½ teaspoon of the ground black pepper, and toss them until the chicken is well coated and there are no seasonings remaining in the bowl.

Melt 4 tablespoons of the butter with the olive oil in a large heavy skillet over medium heat. Once the foaming has subsided, add the chicken, and cook it for 3 minutes, being careful not to let the chicken brown. Flip the chicken pieces and cook them for an additional 3 minutes, until they are fully cooked through. Transfer the chicken to a serving platter and set it aside.

Add the shallots and garlic to the pan, and let them cook for 2 minutes, until the shallots just become translucent. Add the wine and the lemon juice, turn the heat to high, and deglaze the pan of its brown bits with a spatula. Bring the mixture to a boil. Once it's at a full boil, let the mixture boil for 3 additional minutes, or until it becomes thick and syrupy. Add the chicken stock, the remaining ½ teaspoon salt, and ¼ teaspoon pepper. Bring the sauce to a full boil again, and let it boil for an additional 3 minutes.

Remove the pan from the heat, whisk in the remaining 4 tablespoons cold butter, and add the parsley. Pour the sauce over the chicken, garnish it with the lemon slices and wedges, and serve.

Perfect Corn Sticks or Cornbread

Makes 24 sticks or 1 (9 by 13-inch), baking pan

1 cup all-purpose flour
1 cup yellow cornmeal
1 teaspoon salt
1 tablespoon baking powder
¼ teaspoon baking soda
2 large eggs
2 cups buttermilk
8 tablespoons (1 stick) butter, melted

Preheat the oven to 425°F.

In a large bowl, whisk together the flour, cornmeal, salt, baking powder, and baking soda. Crack the eggs into a measuring cup with the buttermilk and lightly whisk them together. Pour the buttermilk-egg mixture and the melted butter into the bowl, and stir everything together until the batter is just combined.

Butter the corn stick molds for the corn sticks or a 9 by 13-inch baking pan for the cornbread. Transfer the batter to the prepared dish or skillet and bake the cornbread for 20 to 25 minutes, until it is golden brown and starts to pull away from the sides of the baking dish. Remove the corn sticks or cornbread from the pan and set them on a cooling rack for at least 15 minutes before slicing and serving. Serve warm or cold.

Tagine of Lamb with Apricots and Almonds

Makes 10 to 12 servings

4 pounds lamb shoulder, cut into 3 ½- to 4-inch cubes
2½ teaspoons salt, divided
1½ teaspoons ground black pepper, divided
2 tablespoons plus 1 teaspoon ground cumin
1 tablespoon plus ½ teaspoon ground ginger
2¼ teaspoons ground turmeric
2 teaspoons paprika
1¼ teaspoons ground cinnamon
4 tablespoons minced garlic, divided
6 tablespoons olive oil
4 tablespoons (½ stick) butter
3 large yellow onions, diced
1 cup diced dried apricots
1 cup diced dried dates
The grated zest of 1 lemon
The grated zest of 1 orange
5 cups beef stock
2¼ teaspoons saffron threads, crumbled
3 tablespoons freshly squeezed lemon juice
The leaves of 1 bunch cilantro, chopped, for garnish
Rice or couscous, for serving
½ cup sliced almonds, toasted, for garnish

In a large bowl, combine the lamb, 2 teaspoons of the salt, 1 teaspoon of the black pepper, the cumin, ginger, turmeric, paprika, cinnamon, and 1 tablespoon of the garlic. Toss these ingredients together so that the lamb is fully coated with every morsel of the seasonings and garlic. Cover the bowl, and let the lamb rest at room temperature for at least 30 minutes, but preferably 2 to 3 hours, so it can absorb the seasonings.

In a large heavy stockpot (4 quarts) or Dutch oven over medium-high heat, combine 4 tablespoons of the olive oil with 1 tablespoon of the butter. When the butter has melted and the foaming has subsided, add the lamb—in batches, if necessary, to avoid overcrowding the pot. Brown the lamb, transferring the cubes to a plate when they are finished. Add the remaining 2 tablespoons olive oil, and 3 tablespoons butter to the pot, and when the foaming has subsided, add the onions and the remaining 3 tablespoons of garlic. Sauté them together until the onions soften, approximately 5 minutes. Add the apricots, dates, orange and lemon zests, and the remaining ½ teaspoon salt and ½ teaspoon ground black pepper. Stir the pot to combine the ingredients thoroughly.

Let the mixture cook for another 5 minutes until the onions are translucent but not browned. Add the browned lamb, the beef stock, crumbled saffron threads, and lemon juice, and turn the heat up to high to bring the mixture to a boil before turning the heat down to let the tagine simmer, just below boiling. Let the tagine simmer, uncovered, for 30 minutes until the liquid has reduced by about one-quarter, and has thickened slightly. Remove the tagine from the heat and let it cool, then refrigerate it, covered, for at least 4 hours, but preferably overnight, or up to 3 days. Reheat the tagine by bringing it to a full boil again before serving it over rice or couscous, garnished with the cilantro and toasted almonds.

This recipe is inspired by my dear friend Gail Marcus Monaghan, who has written a ton of books, and gives super-exclusive cooking classes in New York City.

To-Die-For Ale-Braised Brisket

Makes 8 to 10 servings

1 (4 pound) flat-cut beef brisket, untrimmed
2½ teaspoons salt
1¼ teaspoons ground black pepper
3 tablespoons minced garlic
¼ cup Dijon mustard
¼ cup dark brown sugar, firmly packed
1 tablespoon peeled and grated fresh ginger
2 tablespoons butter
2 medium yellow onions, thinly sliced
1 bay leaf
1 (750-ml) bottle Guinness Stout or
    any other rich dark beer
4 cups beef or chicken stock

Preheat the oven to broil. In a large bowl, combine the brisket, salt, pepper, garlic, Dijon mustard, brown sugar, and ginger, and toss them together until the brisket is fully coated with all of the seasonings.

Melt the butter in a large heavy saucepan over medium high heat. When the foaming has subsided, add the onions, and sauté them for 5 to 7 minutes until they are just beginning to soften.

Place the brisket in a large deep baking dish, scraping the bottom of the bowl to collect all of the seasonings. Add the sautéed onions all around and on top of the brisket, and then add the bay leaf. Pour the stout and stock over the brisket and place it, uncovered, under the broiler. Let it broil for 17 minutes, before turning the oven down to 350°F. After reducing the heat, let it roast, uncovered, for another 43 minutes, 1 hour in total from when you put it in to broil. After an hour, remove the brisket from the oven and cover it tightly with aluminum foil. Return the covered brisket to the oven and let it roast for another 1 hour and 20 minutes before removing it from the oven. Let it rest, covered, for 20 to 25 minutes before slicing and serving.

Perfect Creamed Spinach

Makes 8 to 10 servings

3 tablespoons butter
3 pounds fresh spinach
3 cups heavy cream
1 teaspoon salt
¾ teaspoon ground black pepper
2¼ teaspoons minced garlic
⅜ teaspoon ground nutmeg
1½ cups plus 2 tablespoons grated
    Parmesan cheese, divided

Melt the butter in a large, heavy stockpot over high heat. When the foaming has subsided, add the spinach all at once, and press it down. When the spinach has released its liquid, remove the stockpot from the heat, drain it, and set the spinach aside. This step, over high heat, will take 5 minutes at the most.

Preheat the oven to 350°F. Butter a 9 by 13-inch baking dish. In another large Dutch oven or saucepan combine the cream, salt, pepper, garlic, and nutmeg and bring them to a boil. Turn off the heat, and vigorously whisk in 1 ½ cups of the Parmesan cheese until the sauce is smooth. Add the spinach, and stir it well to combine.

Transfer the spinach mixture to the prepared baking dish, top it with the remaining 2 tablespoons of Parmesan cheese, and bake it in the preheated oven for 20 to 25 minutes, until it's golden brown and bubbly.

Rosemary Roasted Potatoes

Makes 8 to 10 servings

2 pounds fingerling potatoes, quartered or sliced into
⁣   ¾ inch slices
1¼ teaspoons salt
½ teaspoon ground black pepper
1 tablespoon minced garlic
4 tablespoons olive oil
2 tablespoons chopped fresh rosemary leaves

Preheat the oven to 450°F. Combine the ingredients in a large bowl and toss them together thoroughly. Place the potatoes on a large rimmed baking sheet, using a rubber spatula to scrape out all the oil and seasonings from the bowl. Place the baking sheet in the oven and roast the potatoes for 30 minutes, until they are brown and crisp. Serve them immediately.

Broccoli and Cheddar Gratin

Makes 10 to 12 servings

2 tablespoons plus ¾ teaspoon salt, divided
2 pounds broccoli, both florets and stems,
⁣   coarsely chopped
¼ cup plus 2 tablespoons sour cream
1½ cups heavy cream
2¼ cups milk
2 tablespoons butter
½ cup white wine
⅜ teaspoon white pepper
½ teaspoon ground black pepper
¼ teaspoon ground nutmeg
1 tablespoon minced garlic
½ cup plus 2 tablespoons grated Parmesan cheese
2 cups grated sharp Cheddar cheese, firmly packed
3 eggs
¾ teaspoon cracked black pepper

Bring 6 quarts of water to a boil in a large stockpot with 2 tablespoons of the salt. Add the broccoli, and cook it until it's tender but still slightly al dente, about 4 minutes. Drain the broccoli into a colander and let it sit for 10 minutes so as much water as possible can drain from it. Preheat the oven to 350°F. Butter a 9 by 13-inch baking dish.

Set the same large stockpot over a medium-low heat, and add the sour cream, heavy cream, milk, butter, wine, white pepper, black pepper, nutmeg, garlic, and the remaining ¾ teaspoon salt. Bring the mixture to a full boil, turn off the heat, and add ½ cup of the Parmesan cheese and 1½ cups of the cheddar cheese. Whisk the sauce vigorously until the cheeses are melted and fully incorporated, and then let it cool for 5 minutes before whisking in the eggs, one at a time.

Place the broccoli in the prepared baking dish, and pour the cheese mixture over it. Top the dish with the remaining ½ cup Cheddar cheese, 2 tablespoons Parmesan, and the cracked black pepper, and bake it until the gratin is golden brown and bubbly, 35 to 40 minutes.

Easy Oven-Baked Potato Chips

Makes about 150 chips

2 pounds medium Russet potatoes
3½ teaspoons salt, divided
1 teaspoon ground black pepper
1¼ cups olive oil

Preheat the oven to 325°F. Slice the potatoes lengthwise on a mandolin to ⅛-inch thickness. Place 2 quarts water in a large bowl with 1 teaspoon of the salt, and let the sliced potatoes sit for 30 minutes in the bowl to rinse the starch from them. Drain the potatoes into a colander, and then dry them thoroughly with a towel. Return the dry potatoes to the colander. Season them with 2¼ teaspoons of the salt and the black pepper, gently toss them, and let them sit until they have released any remaining liquid, approximately 10 to 15 more minutes.

While the potatoes are draining, brush as many baking sheets as you have, up to five, or in batches, with 4 tablespoons of olive oil each. Place the oiled pans in the preheated oven for 10 minutes. Shake off any excess water from the potatoes draining in the colander and separate them so that they are not sticking together. Remove the sheet pans from the oven, one at a time, and place a layer of potatoes on each of the hot pans, making sure the potatoes are not touching. Bake them in the oven for 10 minutes, then turn them, and bake them for another 5 minutes until they are fully cooked and browned. Remove the chips to a cooling rack, season them with the remaining ¼ teaspoon salt, and let them cool before serving.

Serve them on their own, still warm from the oven or cooled, plain, or get creative and serve them with smoked salmon and crème fraîche as a first course, or with as much good-quality caviar as you can afford as an hors d'oeuvre. Plain or fancy, there's is no way to go wrong with these!

Risotto alla Milanese

Makes 10 to 12 servings

12 tablespoons (1½ sticks) butter
1 medium yellow or white onion, minced
1½ cups Arborio rice
5 cups plus 4 tablespoons rich chicken stock, divided
1½ teaspoons saffron threads
2 tablespoons freshly squeezed lemon juice
1⅛ teaspoons salt
¾ teaspoon ground black pepper
¼ teaspoon cracked black pepper
½ cup plus 2 tablespoons grated Parmesan cheese

Melt 6 tablespoons of the butter in a large Dutch oven over medium heat. When the foaming has subsided, add the onion, and let it soften until it becomes translucent, 8 to 10 minutes. Add the rice and stir to combine fully before adding 5 cups of the chicken stock. Turn the heat to high, and bring the mixture to a boil before covering it and turning the heat to low. Let the rice cook for 25 minutes, stirring it frequently.

In a small bowl, soften the saffron in the remaining 4 tablespoons of chicken stock.

Remove the risotto from the heat, and stir in the remaining 6 tablespoons of butter, the softened saffron and chicken stock, the lemon juice, the salt, both peppers, and the Parmesan cheese. Return the risotto to medium heat, letting it cook for 5 more minutes. You can serve the risotto immediately, but it will stay warm, covered, for up to 25 minutes without reheating.

Foolproof Bourbon-Pecan Pralines

Makes 24 pralines

1½ cups pecans
1½ teaspoons salt, divided
4 tablespoons (½ stick) butter
1½ cups firmly packed light brown sugar
½ cup heavy cream
2 tablespoons pure vanilla extract
1 tablespoon bourbon
1½ cups confectioners' sugar

Preheat the oven to 350°F. On a medium baking sheet, toss the pecans with ¼ teaspoon of the salt. Toast the pecans for 6 to 8 minutes, until they have a palpably nutty aroma. Remove the pecans from the oven and set them aside. Line 2 large baking sheets with parchment paper.

In a large heavy saucepan over medium heat, melt the butter, brown sugar, heavy cream, vanilla, bourbon, and the remaining 1¼ teaspoons salt. When the butter has melted, and the sugar has dissolved, turn the heat to high, and bring the mixture to a boil. Once the mixture has reached a full boil, let it boil on high heat for 1 minute. Immediately turn the heat down to medium-high. Working quickly, whisk in the powdered sugar a little at time until it's smooth, then continue to beat the mixture vigorously for an additional 30 seconds. Remove it from the heat and stir in the pecans. Using a large metal spoon, scoop out 2 to 3 pecans with the caramel and place them onto the parchment-lined baking sheets creating rough rounds approximately 1½ to 2 inches in diameter. Let the pralines cool for 15 to 20 minutes, until they are set. Serve them after dinner with coffee—if you can resist them that long.

Bourbon Whipped Cream

I always think of Lee Bailey whenever I make this recipe.

Makes 1½ cups, 10 to 12 servings

1 cup heavy cream
¼ cup sugar
1 pinch salt
2 tablespoons high-quality bourbon, see Note

Combine all of the ingredients in the bowl of an electric stand mixer fitted with the whisk attachment. Whip them on medium speed until soft peaks form. Serve this over everything!

Note: Even with all of the new and fancy offerings, I still love Maker's Mark or Wild Turkey.

"Devotedly, Betty's" Tipsy Ambrosia

Makes 4 cups; 10 to 12 servings

9 navel oranges, peeled, and sectioned
9 grapefruits, peeled, and sectioned
½ cup shredded coconut
½ cup toasted almonds
½ cup sugar
⅛ teaspoon salt
4 tablespoons high-quality bourbon
4 tablespoons Grand Marnier

Combine all of the ingredients in a large bowl, stir them well so that they are fully combined, and cover them with plastic wrap. Refrigerate them for at least 8 hours and up to 3 days before serving.

Connie's Chocolate Sauce

Connie Wald was a dear friend in Los Angeles who served absolutely delicious everything.

Makes 1 cup

4 ounces unsweetened chocolate, chopped
1 tablespoon butter
1 cup sugar
¼ teaspoon salt
½ cup half-and-half
1 tablespoon pure vanilla extract

Melt the chocolate and butter in a double boiler over medium-low heat. In a medium bowl, whisk together the sugar, salt, and half-and-half. Add the sugar-cream mixture to the chocolate-butter mixture, and cook it over the double boiler until the sugar has fully dissolved. Stir in the vanilla and serve the sauce warm over vanilla ice cream, or just about anything else.

LEFT: *My mother's mother, Betty Moseley, 1932, in a hand-colored photo that she sent to my grandfather before they married, signed, "Devotedly, Betty."*

Grand Marnier Soufflé with Vanilla Grand Marnier Sauce

Makes 8 servings

1 tablespoon cold butter
1 cup plus 5 tablespoons sugar, divided, plus
   1½ tablespoons sugar for the dish
6 egg yolks
¾ teaspoon salt, divided
¼ cup plus 2 tablespoons Grand Marnier
The zest of 1 navel orange
9 egg whites
Vanilla Grand Marnier Sauce, recipe follows, for serving

Preheat the oven to 400°F. Butter an 8-cup soufflé dish using all of the butter. Sprinkle 1½ tablespoons sugar into the dish, invert it, and make sure the sugar fully coats the buttered surface.

In the bowl of an electric stand mixer fitted with the whisk attachment, combine the egg yolks, 1 cup plus 2 tablespoons of the sugar, and ½ teaspoon of the salt, and beat them together on the highest speed for 10 minutes. Stop the mixer and scrape the sides of the bowl with a rubber spatula. Combine the Grand Marnier and orange zest, and pour them into the bowl. Beat the mixture on high speed for an additional 12 minutes until it is pale, thick, and frothy.

Transfer the egg yolk mixture to a large bowl and clean the stand mixer bowl. Add the egg whites, the remaining ¼ teaspoon salt, and the remaining 3 tablespoons sugar to the bowl and gradually beat the whites on low to medium to high speed for 5 to 7 minutes until soft peaks form. Add one quarter of the egg whites to the egg yolks and blend them well. Fold in the remaining egg whites carefully so as not to deflate the mixture. Gently transfer the mixture to the prepared soufflé dish, place it on a baking sheet, and put it in the preheated oven.

Lower the oven temperature to 375°F, and bake the soufflé until it is fully risen and brown on top, 25 to 30 minutes. Serve it immediately with Vanilla Grand Marnier Sauce.

Note: I always undercook soufflés because I love them when they "self-sauce." The crust combined with an undercooked interior is, to me, a magnificent combination. Do not be intimidated by the concept of making a soufflé—this one could not be easier.

VANILLA GRAND MARNIER SAUCE
Makes 2 cups

2 cups heavy cream
1½ cups sugar
1 tablespoon vanilla extract
1 teaspoon salt
3 tablespoons Grand Marnier
The zest of ½ navel orange

Whisk all the ingredients together in a heavy saucepan over medium heat. Slowly bring them to a boil, then turn off the heat. Strain the sauce through a fine sieve. Serve it warm or cold.

THE ABSOLUTELY-PERFECT-EVERY-TIME THANKSGIVING

BLUE CHEESE COINS

PUMPKIN SOUP WITH APPLES
AND ROSEMARY

PERFECT ROAST TURKEY WITH
SHERRY AND GIBLET GRAVY

AUNT BETTY'S
ORANGE CRANBERRY SAUCE

DOROTHY'S CORNBREAD DRESSING

BAKED SWEET POTATOES
WITH BANANAS

OVEN-ROASTED BRUSSELS SPROUTS

GEORGIA PECAN TARTS

MY MOTHER'S FRENCH SILK PIE

CONNIE'S—AND—AUDREY'S—AND—
ALEX'S APPLE CONFIT

With the exception of the holidays, the majority of Americans have so many already prepared food options that they rarely cook anymore: no time, too much trouble, rather'd be doing something else. But holiday time is different, and steeped in traditions, be they beloved and good, or beloved but bad—to me, no offense, but the marshmallows on the sweet potatoes and green bean casserole made with canned soup both go in the beloved but bad category. These are the rare times for families to still cook together. Remember the cheap wine commercial from years ago, "If you're not sure about the people, be sure about the wine?" That's the way I feel about these recipes. Who knows about your family, but these recipes are bulletproof, foolproof, surefire hits—with the only exception being the cooking time of the turkey, because everyone's oven is different, and only you know your oven. In the essential spirit of convivial family fellowship, I had a friend tell me that he always loves making my recipes for holidays for the simple reason that they make his dreaded sister-in-law, who fancies herself a gourmet, really jealous.

Dorothy Williams Davis was our cook in Atlanta for more than 40 years. I love this photo of her all dolled up in New York at my brother Thomas' wedding, fall 2004.

Dorothy was our fantastic cook for more than forty years, and her dressing is a superb, easy but complexly-flavored one that I had every year growing up. Hers used a different cornbread but this nothing-to-it version is my favorite of the more than forty cornbreads I've developed. Aunt Betty was my father's younger sister, who appreciated great food but wasn't disposed to spend hours and hours achieving it. New York hostess and decorator—and fabulous cook—Susan Gutfreund inspired me to put bananas in the sweet potatoes, and the result is far greater than the sum of its parts. My mother loved all things French, and silk, hence her affinity for this easy, splendid, and decadent French silk pie, a staple at our Thanksgiving table, and Connie Wald credited Audrey Hepburn, her very best friend in the world, for this magnificent confit of apples, which she would serve both with her turkeys in Beverly Hills, and over vanilla ice cream afterwards.

Blue Cheese Coins

Makes 36 coins

6 tablespoons (¾ stick) butter, softened
4 ounces Stilton blue cheese, crumbled
¼ teaspoon ground black pepper
¾ cup all-purpose flour
¼ teaspoon cracked black pepper
¼ teaspoon salt

In an electric stand mixer fitted with the paddle attachment, beat the butter, Stilton, and ground black pepper on medium speed until they are smooth. Add the flour and mix them until they are just combined. Do not overmix.

Shape the dough into a log, about 1¾ inches in diameter. Wrap the dough in plastic wrap, and let it chill for at least 4 hours and up to 24.

When you're ready to bake the coins, preheat the oven to 375°F, and line 2 heavy baking sheets with parchment paper. Cut the log into ¼-inch-thick slices. Place the slices 2 inches apart on the prepared baking sheets. Sprinkle the coins with the cracked black pepper.

Bake the coins in batches until they are golden, about 10 minutes. Remove the coins from the oven, season them with the salt, and let them cool in the pans for 5 minutes. Transfer them to a cooling rack and let them cool completely, about 20 minutes. The coins will keep for about a week in an airtight container, but they can be frozen for up to 6 months.

Pumpkin Soup with Apples and Rosemary

Makes 3 quarts, 12 to 15 servings

4 tablespoons (½ stick) butter
2 onions, peeled and diced
4 carrots, peeled and diced
2 apples, peeled and diced
2 tablespoons chopped fresh rosemary leaves
4 cups pure pumpkin puree, canned—make sure
    it's not pie filling!
6 cups chicken stock
2 teaspoons salt
½ teaspoon ground white pepper
2 cups heavy cream

Melt the butter in a medium-sized stockpot over medium heat. When the foaming has subsided, add the onion, carrot, apple, and rosemary and sauté them until they are tender, 12 to 15 minutes.

Transfer the mixture to the bowl of a food processor fitted with the metal blade, and puree it until it's completely smooth. Return the puree to the stockpot, add the pumpkin puree and chicken stock, and stir until everything is thoroughly combined. Return the mixture to medium heat and simmer the soup for 15 minutes, until it is fully heated through. Add the cream and stir, simmering, for 5 more minutes. Do not let the soup boil. Serve it immediately, or let it cool and refrigerate it for up to 3 days, covered, before reheating it later over low heat.

Perfect Roast Turkey with Sherry and Giblet Gravy

Makes 12 to 15 servings

16 tablespoons (2 sticks) butter, at room temperature
3 cloves garlic, minced, plus 6 whole cloves
2 shallots, minced
1 (12-pound) turkey, fully thawed and
    at room temperature
1 tablespoon plus 1¾ teaspoons salt
1 tablespoon ground black pepper
6 tablespoons chopped fresh sage
2 lemons, halved
1 medium onion, peeled and sliced into 8 wedges
2 cups white wine

Preheat the oven to 325°F. Combine the butter, minced garlic, and shallots in a medium bowl. Remove the giblets, kidneys, and neck, and set them aside in the refrigerator; they will be used later for the gravy. Place the turkey in a very large bowl, add the salt, pepper, and sage, and turn the turkey in the bowl to ensure it is completely covered with the seasonings. If there are excess seasonings at the bottom of the bowl, rub them on the turkey again, making certain that every morsel of salt, pepper, and sage is applied to the turkey.

Place the turkey in a large heavy roasting pan and squeeze the lemons over it. Reapply any seasonings that fall off. Smear the butter over the top of the turkey fully covering the top and wings. Place the squeezed lemons, the onion, and the whole garlic cloves inside the cavity, and pour the wine into the bottom of the roasting pan. Cover the pan tightly with aluminum foil, and place it in the oven.

Roast the turkey for 2½ hours, then remove it from the oven. Turn the oven up to 425°F, remove the foil, and roast the turkey for 30 to 45 minutes more, until the skin is golden brown, and the turkey reaches 155°F on a meat thermometer. Total roasting time should be approximately 15 minutes per pound. When it has reached 155°F, remove it from the oven and transfer it to a carving board. Let the turkey rest for 25 minutes before carving it.

SHERRY AND GIBLET GRAVY
Makes 2½ cups

1 large onion, chopped
The turkey giblets, kidneys, and neck, coarsely
    chopped
¾ cup dry sherry
1¾ cups chicken stock

Place the roasting pan with all of its juices on the stovetop over medium-high heat. Once it's bubbling, add the onion, giblets, kidneys, and neck. Sauté them for 8 to 10 minutes, until everything starts to brown, and then add the sherry to deglaze the pan, scraping the bottom with a metal spatula or wooden spoon to capture all the browned bits. Be very thorough. Add the chicken stock, and turn the heat to high. Boil the gravy until it reduces by about one-third, 7 to 9 minutes.

Strain the sauce through a sieve into a bowl and discard the solids. Skim as much fat as you can from the reserved sauce. Spoon it generously over the carved turkey, and transfer the remaining sauce to a gravy boat to serve alongside the turkey.

My father's sister, Aunt Betty, as a debutante, Atlanta, 1947.

Aunt Betty's Orange Cranberry Relish

Makes 2 cups, 12 to 15 servings

2 cups fresh cranberries (approximately one 12-ounce bag)
1 medium navel orange, cut into 8 wedges—
     use the whole thing!
¼ cup sugar
¼ teaspoon ground cinnamon
2 tablespoons Grand Marnier

Place the ingredients in the bowl of a food processor fitted with the metal blade and process them until they are combined but still chunky with a relish consistency.

Dorothy's Cornbread Dressing

Makes 12 to 15 servings

1 pound bulk pork sausage
6 tablespoons (¾ stick) butter, plus 4 tablespoons
     melted butter
1½ cups chopped onions
1 cup chopped celery
1½ cups finely diced carrots
1 tablespoon minced garlic
½ cup minced shallot
½ pound medium button mushrooms, sliced
1 teaspoon salt
¾ teaspoon ground black pepper
Perfect Cornbread, page 44
2½ cups chicken stock
3 eggs, lightly beaten
¼ teaspoon ground sage
1 teaspoon dried thyme
¼ teaspoon ground nutmeg
¼ cup dry sherry

Preheat the oven to 375°F. Butter a 9 by 13-inch baking dish. Brown the sausage in a large heavy skillet over medium heat, breaking it up with a spatula. Once it's fully cooked through, remove the pan from the heat. Pour off the fat if there is any, and reserve the browned sausage.

Melt 6 tablespoons of the butter in another large heavy skillet over medium heat. When the foaming has subsided, add the onions, celery, carrots, garlic, shallots, mushrooms, salt, and pepper, and sauté them until they are soft, 10 to 15 minutes.

In a large bowl, break the cornbread into small pieces and then add the browned sausage, sautéed vegetables, chicken stock, eggs, sage, thyme, nutmeg, sherry, and melted butter. Stir the mixture to combine or, better yet, mix all the ingredients with your hands so that everything is fully combined before putting the mixture in the prepared dish. Bake the dressing for 30 to 40 minutes, until it is golden brown and crusty on top. Let it rest at least 5 minutes before serving, or it may be cooled, covered, and refrigerated for up to 4 days before reheating it, covered, for serving.

Baked Sweet Potatoes with Bananas

Makes 12 to 15 servings

12 medium sweet potatoes
4 bananas
12 tablespoons (1½ sticks) butter, divided
1 egg, beaten
6 tablespoons dry sherry
¾ teaspoon salt
¼ teaspoon ground black pepper
⅛ teaspoon ground nutmeg
¼ teaspoon ground cinnamon
¼ cup chopped pecans

Preheat the oven to 450°F.

Scrub and dry the sweet potatoes. Place them on a baking sheet and bake them until they are tender when pierced with a fork, about 1 hour. Remove the sweet potatoes from the oven and reduce the oven temperature to 350°F.

Butter a 9 by 13-inch baking dish.

Once the sweet potatoes are cool enough to handle, remove their skins, and place them into the bowl of an electric stand mixer fitted with the paddle attachment. Peel the bananas, and add them to the sweet potatoes with 11 tablespoons of the butter. Mash them together with a fork. Add the egg, sherry, salt, pepper, nutmeg, and cinnamon to the sweet potatoes and then beat on medium speed until they are light and fluffy, 3 to 4 minutes.

Scoop the mixture into the prepared dish, dot it with the remaining tablespoon of butter, and the chopped pecans. Place the dish in the oven, and bake it for 20 to 25 minutes, until the sweet potatoes are fully heated through. Serve them immediately, or let them cool, covered and refrigerated, up to 3 days in advance. When you're ready to serve, reheat them, covered, at 325°F for about 30 minutes.

Oven-Roasted Brussels Sprouts

Makes 12 to 15 servings

3 pounds brussels sprouts, scored with a cross
    at the stem, brown leaves removed
¾ teaspoon salt
¼ teaspoon plus ⅛ teaspoon ground black pepper
¾ cup olive oil

Preheat the oven to 375°F. Line a large baking sheet with parchment paper.

Toss the brussels sprouts in a large bowl with the salt, pepper, and olive oil. Use a rubber spatula to scrape the seasoned brussels sprouts onto the prepared baking sheet, being sure to capture all of the seasonings and oil. Bake them for 30 to 45 minutes, until they are ever-so-slightly browned and tender all the way through when pierced with a knife. Serve them immediately.

Georgia Pecan Tarts

Makes 12 servings

FOR THE CRUST:
16 tablespoons (2 sticks) cold butter
1½ cups dark brown sugar, firmly packed
2 cups all-purpose flour
½ teaspoon salt

FOR THE PECAN TOPPING:
4 large eggs
1½ cups dark brown sugar, firmly packed
1 tablespoon plus 1 teaspoon vanilla extract
½ teaspoon salt
1½ cups chopped pecans

Preheat the oven to 350°F. Butter a 9 by 13-inch metal baking pan.

TO MAKE THE CRUST:
In the bowl of an electric stand mixer fitted with the paddle attachment, cream the butter and sugar together on medium speed until they have lightened in color and texture, about 5 minutes. Turn the speed to low and add the flour and salt, mixing them until you have coarse crumbs. Pour the crumbs into the prepared baking pan, and press them down with your fingers to cover the pan evenly. Bake the crust for 20 minutes, until it is just brown, and let it cool completely. Keep the oven on.

TO MAKE THE PECAN TOPPING:
Add the eggs, brown sugar, vanilla extract, and salt to a large mixing bowl and whisk them together until they are just combined. Do not over-whisk them or the tart will be dry. Stir in the chopped pecans.

TO ASSEMBLE THE TART:
Pour the pecan topping over the cooled crust and bake the tart for 20 minutes until it is just set. Remove the tart from the oven, and let it cool for at least 30 minutes before slicing it. Serve the tart with Perfect French Vanilla Ice Cream, page 146, or Bourbon Whipped Cream, page 183.

Connie's–and–Audrey's– and–Alex's Apple Confit

Makes 12 servings

10 Red Delicious or Granny Smith apples,
    whichever look better
8 tablespoons (1 stick) butter
1 medium onion, halved and sliced thinly
    into half-moons
3½ cups sugar
1¼ teaspoons salt
3 tablespoons freshly squeezed lemon juice
1 teaspoon ground nutmeg
2½ teaspoons ground cinnamon
½ teaspoon ground cloves
1 cup brandy

Peel, core, and cut each apple into 8 wedges. In a large
heavy stockpot over medium-low heat, melt the butter.
When the foaming has subsided, add the onions, and
cook them until they are translucent and softened, but
not colored, approximately 15 to 20 minutes.

Add the apples, sugar, salt, lemon juice, nutmeg, cinnamon, cloves, and brandy, and turn the heat all the way
up until the mixture just starts to bubble. Turn it down
to a very low simmer, and let the apples cook for
2½ hours, until they are completely soft and there
is only a very syrupy mixture still in the pan that has
become very dark brown in color. Remove the mixture
from the heat, let it cool, and refrigerate it overnight.
The following day, or up to 4 days later, reheat the
confit very slowly on low before serving it alongside
your turkey, or over vanilla ice cream.

*My dear friend, Connie Wald, with her dearest friend, Audrey
Hepburn, Switzerland, 1969. Connie always said she "stole" this recipe
from Audrey—I added the onion, but the foundation was theirs.*

My Mother's French Silk Pie

Makes 12 servings

Perfect-Every-Time Pâte Brisée, page 27
8 ounces unsweetened chocolate, divided
2 teaspoons espresso powder
3 sticks (¾ pound) butter, at room temperature
2¼ cups sugar
1 tablespoon plus 1 teaspoon vanilla extract
3 tablespoons Grand Marnier
1 teaspoon salt
6 eggs
Bourbon Whipped Cream, page 52

Melt 6 ounces of the chocolate with the espresso powder in a heavy saucepan or a double boiler over low heat. Stir them together until the chocolate is smooth. Set the chocolate aside to let it cool completely.

Place the butter and sugar in the bowl of an electric stand mixer fitted with the paddle attachment, and beat them on medium high until they are light and fluffy, 6 to 7 minutes. Add the cooled chocolate-espresso mixture, vanilla, Grand Marnier, and salt, and beat the mixture until everything is fully incorporated. Add 3 of the eggs, one at a time, and beat the mixture for an additional 5 minutes. Add the last 3 eggs, one at a time, and beat the mixture for another 5 minutes. Using a rubber spatula, pour the filling into the cooled crust.

Chop the remaining 2 ounces of chocolate. Sprinkle the top of the pie with one-half of the chopped chocolate, cover it with plastic wrap, and let it chill in the refrigerator for at least 6 hours, preferably overnight. Before serving, top the pie with the Bourbon Whipped Cream and garnish it with the remaining chopped chocolate.

With my parents in Atlanta, Thanksgiving, 1972.
My outfit certinaly says, "special occasion."

A TOTALLY DO-AHEAD BUT SUPER-SWANKY CHRISTMAS EVE DINNER

BEVERLY HILLS EGG-NOG

SMOKED SALMON GALETTE
WITH CAVIAR

CUCUMBER SALAD WITH RADICCHIO

LOUISE'S SEAFOOD POT PIE

SNOW-WHITE MERINGUES WITH
HOMEMADE PEPPERMINT ICE CREAM
AND CONNIE'S CHOCOLATE SAUCE

When I was growing up in Atlanta, Christmas was all about concerts. That's because my stepfather, Robert Shaw, conducted at least twelve of them every December—a Festival of Carols, with collegiate and children's groups and the Atlanta Symphony Orchestra, and Handel's *Messiah*, with more than three hundred people in the chorus.

Robert was Mr. Christmas. His album *Christmas Hymns and Carols* was the first classical record ever to go "gold," and each year tens of thousands of people heard his concerts live, not to mention the millions more who listened in radioland. Then came the Kennedy Center Honors, an annual pilgrimage to Washington for us starting in 1991, when Robert was made a recipient of that distinguished prize.

The weekend was super-swanky, heady, and so much fun. Every minute was a celebration for the honorees, their families, and Kennedy Center Honors "alums": dinners in the period rooms of the State Department, lunches at the Jockey Club, receptions at The White House, and performances at the Kennedy Center. The awards are billed as honoring "those individuals who made lifetime contributions to American culture through the performing arts," so at each of those events in those years any one of us could have been seated next to Ella Fitzgerald, Lauren Bacall, Katharine Hepburn, Johnny Carson, Ginger Rogers, André Previn, or Jessye Norman to name a few. As glamorous as those Decembers were, by the time Christmas Eve rolled around, we were all, let's say this as nicely as possible, exhausted, and only in the mood for a fairly quiet family celebration.

If we went to church, the dinner at home afterwards would be something elegant and simple—but totally do-aheadable. My mother would serve something like this menu, although this one is actually inspired by Louise Grunwald, a famous New York philanthropist and superb hostess, and a dear friend. As well as anyone, Louise understands the power of chic simplicity when it comes to food. And her tables are so enchanting that you just hate to leave them when her dinners are over.

My Christmases these days are spent either in New York or Los Angeles. If I'm in New York, I'll go to an early service of lessons and carols at St. Thomas Church on Fifth Avenue, and then to the house of a festive friend who serves a very jolly dinner, down to the personalized snow globes as place cards, and Christmas crackers. In L.A., I entertain at home—or go to a friend's house to do the cooking. But we all have our own traditions, and every year they're a bit different, the inevitable clang in the march of time. We all have them in our lives. So take my advice: stick with an easy, appealing, foolproof, and delicious menu, and damn the torpedoes!

TOP: *Robert conducting the Cleveland Orchestra, 1963.*
BOTTOM: *Kennedy Center Honorees with President and Mrs. Bush at the White House, December, 1991.*

Beverly Hills Egg-Nog

12 to 16 servings

12 eggs, separated
2½ cups sugar
1 teaspoon plus a pinch salt, divided
1 teaspoon pure vanilla extract
4 cups (1 quart) excellent-quality bourbon
3 cups heavy cream
Ground nutmeg and cinnamon, for garnish

In the bowl of an electric stand mixer fitted with the whisk attachment, combine the egg yolks, sugar, 1 teaspoon of the salt, the vanilla, and bourbon, and beat them together on medium speed until they are light and fluffy, approximately 3 minutes. Transfer the mixture to a bowl, and stir in the heavy cream, but do not whip it.

Clean and dry the stand mixer's bowl, and add the egg whites. Whip the egg whites on medium speed with the remaining pinch of salt until soft peaks form. Fold the egg whites carefully into the egg yolk mixture and refrigerate the egg-nog covered for at least 4 hours, and up to 3 days, before serving it cold.

Why not go absolutely nuts on Christmas cookies?
Food stylist Torie Cox decorated these. Aren't they fab?

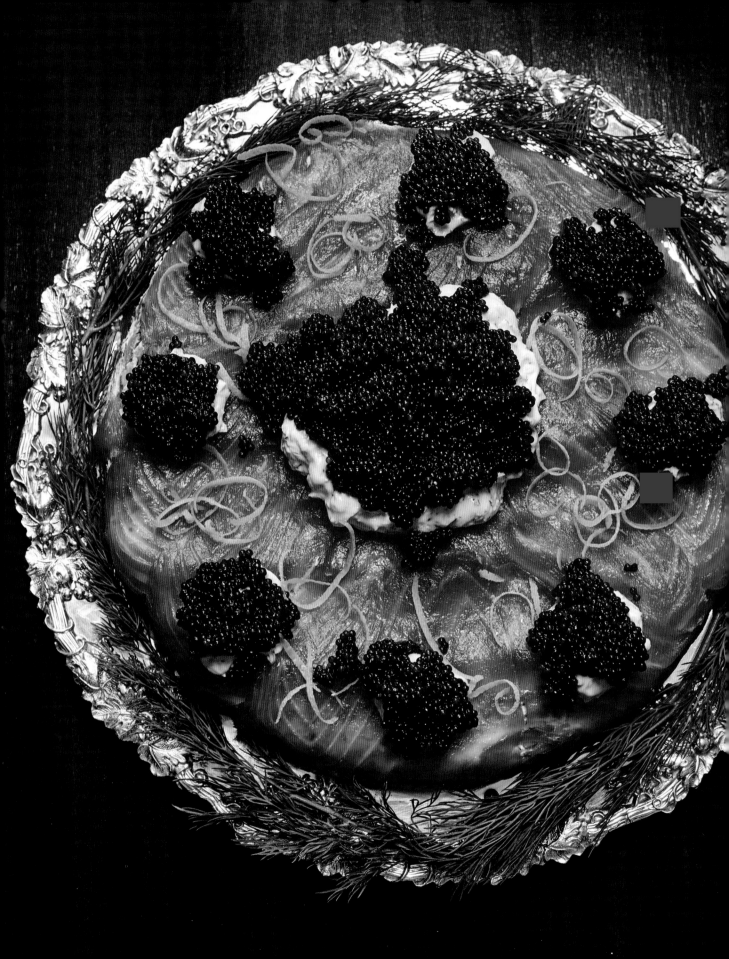

Smoked Salmon Galette with Caviar

Makes 10 to 12 servings

1 pound cream cheese
¼ cup Perfect Homemade Mayonnaise, page 28,
  or Hellman's
¼ cup sour cream
2 large shallots, minced
3 tablespoons plus 1½ teaspoons freshly squeezed
  lemon juice
¼ cup chopped fresh dill
½ teaspoon salt
½ teaspoon ground black pepper
2½ pounds smoked salmon, thinly sliced
Freshly cracked black pepper
As much excellent-quality caviar as you can afford
The zest of 2 lemons, grated then finely chopped,
  for garnish

Line an 8½-inch springform pan with plastic wrap. In the bowl of a stand mixer fitted with the paddle attachment, combine the cream cheese, mayonnaise, sour cream, shallots, 3 tablespoons of the lemon juice, the dill, salt, and ground black pepper, and beat them together for a couple of minutes until they are thoroughly combined, smooth, and spreadable.

Assemble a layer of salmon slices at the bottom of the prepared springform pan, making sure the entire bottom is covered, and placing the pieces so they are facing in the same direction so the finished product will look uniform and gorgeous. Dot the salmon layer with ¼ teaspoon of the remaining lemon juice and some freshly cracked black pepper, and then spread 5 tablespoons of the cream cheese mixture evenly over the layer. Repeat this step until you have six layers, and then press down on the last layer to fully compress the galette. Reserve any excess filling to finish the galette. The excess can be kept in the refrigerator and brought to room temperature before finishing.

Let the galette chill, covered in the refrigerator for at least 2 hours or up to 3 days, before serving. To serve, invert the galette onto a serving platter, top it with the remaining cream cheese mixture, then garnish it with the caviar, lemon zest, and more cracked black pepper. Slice the galette into 10 to 12 wedges, and serve it cold.

Cucumber Salad with Radicchio

Makes 10 to 12 servings

2 English cucumbers, thinly sliced
The Easiest, Best Vinaigrette in the World, page 28
2 tablespoons chopped fresh chives
⅛ teaspoon salt
⅛ teaspoon ground black pepper
2 heads radicchio

Place the cucumber slices into a medium bowl, and add 6 tablespoons of the vinaigrette, the chives, salt, and pepper. Carefully stir the cucumbers to combine them with the seasonings and dressing, but making sure to keep the cucumber slices intact. Cover the bowl and set it in the refrigerator overnight. When you're ready to serve, separate the radicchio leaves, place them on a serving platter as shown on page 88, and place mounds of the cucumber salad on the beds of radicchio leaves.

Louise's Seafood Pot Pie

Makes 10 to 12 servings

12 tablespoons (1½ sticks) butter
3 pounds mixed shellfish, such as finely diced shrimp,
    lobster, scallops, crabmeat, or oysters
2¼ teaspoons salt, divided
1¼ plus ⅛ teaspoons ground black pepper, divided
1½ cups dry vermouth
1 pound medium button mushrooms
2 large shallots, minced
1½ cups milk
1½ cups plus 2 tablespoons heavy cream
½ cup white wine
1 teaspoon dry mustard
4 tablespoons tomato paste
2 teaspoons dried tarragon
4 tablespoons all-purpose flour
1 pound Gruyère cheese, grated
1 (11 by 16-inch) sheet all-butter puff pastry
1 egg

Preheat the oven to 375°F. Butter a 9 by 13-inch baking dish.

Melt 8 tablespoons of the butter in a large heavy stockpot over medium-high heat. When the foaming has subsided, add the seafood, ¾ teaspoon of the salt, and ½ teaspoon of the black pepper, and sauté the seafood approximately 4 to 5 minutes, stirring it constantly with a rubber spatula until it is only partially cooked through. Add the vermouth, and continue to sauté the seafood for another 3 minutes or so until it's just cooked through but still very rare. Drain the seafood in a colander over a bowl, set aside the seafood, and return the liquid to the stockpot. Add the mushrooms, shallots, ¼ teaspoon of the salt, and ⅛ teaspoon of the black pepper, and let the mushrooms and shallots steep in the liquid approximately 5 to 7 minutes, until they are just cooked through, and then drain them into a colander over a bowl. Set aside the vegetables, and return the liquid to the stockpot.

Add the milk, 1½ cups of the heavy cream, the white wine, dry mustard, tomato paste, tarragon, and the remaining 1¼ teaspoons salt and ¾ teaspoon black pepper, and whisk the mixture vigorously to break up the tomato paste. Bring the mixture to a boil, then reduce the heat to low, to allow the sauce to simmer.

In a separate heavy skillet over medium-high heat, melt the remaining 4 tablespoons butter and the flour together to make a roux, and then add it to the milk-cream mixture, again whisking vigorously to break up any lumps. Bring it to a boil and remove it from the heat. Whisk in the cheese a little at a time to make a smooth sauce. Add the cooked seafood and mushrooms to the prepared baking dish, pour the sauce over the seafood and mushrooms, and place the puff pastry on top, trimming the edges to make it neat. *Note:* The pot pie may be assembled up to this point, covered, and refrigerated for up to 3 days before bringing it to room temperature again and baking it.

In a small bowl, beat the egg with the remaining 2 tablespoons heavy cream. Brush the puff pastry with the egg wash, place the baking dish on a sheet pan as there will be overflow from the cheese—incidentally, the browned cheese and sauce is the part I can't ever stop eating—and then place the pot pie in the oven. Bake it for 25 to 30 minutes, until the pastry is golden brown and cooked through. Let the pot pie rest for at least 10 minutes before serving.

Louise, photographed by Horst in New York, 1965.

Snow-White Meringues with Homemade Peppermint Ice Cream and Connie's Chocolate Sauce

Makes 18 (3-inch) meringues, 10 to 12 servings with leftovers

12 egg whites, at room temperature
4 cups superfine sugar
1 tablespoon vanilla extract
½ teaspoon cream of tartar
¾ teaspoon salt
Homemade Peppermint Ice Cream, recipe follows
Connie's Chocolate Sauce, page 55

Preheat the oven to 250°F and line two heavy baking sheets with parchment paper. With a 3-inch circular mold or construction paper, draw 6 circles on each of the pieces of parchment paper, and set the baking sheets aside.

Add all the ingredients to the bowl of a stand mixer and turn the mixer to the highest speed. Let the mixer run until you can hear a palpable change in the tone of the mixer, about 5 or 6 minutes. Check the meringue base to make sure it's thick and fluffy, and not too wet to handle without it falling back on itself. In other words, it should hold very stiff peaks.

With a pastry bag fitted with a large star tip, pipe the meringue in rows into the drawn circles on the parchment paper. A secret: If you're not handy with a pastry bag, just take a rubber spatula and spread the meringue onto the drawn round. The result will be more rustic, but beautiful just the same. Turn the oven down to 200°F, and bake the meringues for 1½ hours.

Turn the oven off, but leave the meringues in the oven overnight. Do not open the oven door until the next morning. They should be perfectly white, and not browned in the least.

Note: The meringues can be stored in an airtight container for up to three days.

Connie Wald and Dominick Dunne at my house in Los Angeles, Fall, 2007.

HOMEMADE PEPPERMINT ICE CREAM
Makes 10 to 12 servings

2 pounds peppermints
2½ cups heavy cream
1½ cups whole milk
1 tablespoon plus 2½ teaspoons pure vanilla extract
8 egg yolks
1 ¼ cups sugar
¾ teaspoon salt
½ teaspoon pure peppermint extract

Place the peppermints in a food processor fitted with a metal blade and pulse them into very small pieces. Transfer the peppermint pieces in a large bowl with the heavy cream, milk, vanilla, egg yolks, sugar, salt, and peppermint extract. Gently stir them together. Pour the mixture in an ice cream maker and proceed according to the manufacturer's instructions. Serve with Connie's Chocolate Sauce.

A BIG WOW OF A BUFFET LUNCH FOR BOXING DAY

BROCCOLI AND CHEDDAR SOUP

SMOKED SALMON WITH
HARD-COOKED EGGS, RED ONION
AND CRÈME FRAÎCHE

STONE-CRAB CLAWS WITH
BEST-EVER MUSTARD SAUCE

STANDING RIB OF ROAST BEEF
WITH HORSERADISH SAUCE
AND YORKSHIRE PUDDING

SLICED IBÉRICO HAM

FETTUCINE WITH BLACK
TRUFFLES AND PARMESAN

AVOCADO, ORANGE,
GRAPEFRUIT, AND RED ONION
SALAD WITH ARUGULA AND
MACADAMIA NUTS

STRAWBERRY POTS-DE-CRÈME WITH
RED FRUIT COULIS

BUTTERSCOTCH WHITE-CHOCOLATE
PECAN COOKIES

COCONUT—RASPBERRY RUM CAKE

In Los Angeles for the past twenty-three years, one of my very favorite parties has been on Boxing Day, the day after Christmas, the traditional day in England for the opening of the boxes. It's a lunch for about one hundred people given by my dear friends Mary Hayley and Selim Zilkha, English and Iraqi ex-pats who came from London to live in L.A. around 1980. They entertain so generously, with such attention to detail and quality—and they do it so often—that it was difficult to decide which of their parties is my favorite. But after careful consideration, I chose their Boxing Day buffet lunch—a lollapalooza of family—adopted and natural—and friends from around the world, and straightforward, delicious, glamorous food,

set on pastel-colored tables in their sunny citrus garden overlooking Bel-Air. It's splashy and fun, and, in the zillions of times they have invited me to their parties over the years, I've yet to have had anything but a stellar time.

As this book was shot in Atlanta and not Mary and Selim's sunny citrus garden, I combined theses—a menu inspired by their actual Boxing Day lunch with a few additions—many dishes you can do ahead and many you can just buy and gussy-up without the trouble of actual cooking—and the decorating sensibility of my mother. She hated the idea of winter and Christmas so much that sometimes as early as 6:30 in the morning on December 26, she'd have all of the gold, red, piney wreaths, boughs, and trees hauled out, and would fill the house with daffodils, tulips, peonies, or anything else that might give her hope that winter was on the wane and spring was coming.

ABOVE: *Selim Zilkha and Mary Hayley, Los Angeles, 1990.*
RIGHT: *Just call Kirk Whitfield in Atlanta whenever you want a fab arrangement like this.*

Broccoli and Cheddar Soup

Makes 6 to 8 servings or 24 small shot glasses

2 tablespoons butter
2 large shallots, chopped
1½ teaspoons minced garlic
1 cup white wine, divided
1½ cups milk
1¼ cups heavy cream
¾ cup chicken stock
2⅛ teaspoons salt
¼ teaspoon white pepper
½ teaspoon ground black pepper
¼ teaspoon ground nutmeg
2 tablespoons golden sherry
1 cup shredded Cheddar cheese, firmly packed
¼ cup plus 2 tablespoons grated Parmesan cheese
1½ pounds broccoli, blanched in
    salted water and pureed
2 tablespoons chopped fresh dill, for garnish

Melt the butter in a large heavy stockpot over medium heat. When the foaming has subsided, add the shallots and garlic, and sauté them until they are translucent, 4 to 5 minutes. Add ½ cup of the white wine, turn the heat up to high, and let the mixture reduce by half, 4 to 5 minutes more. Add the remaining ½ cup wine, the milk, heavy cream, chicken stock, salt, both peppers, nutmeg, and sherry, and return the mixture to a boil.

Turn off the heat, and whisk in the Cheddar and Parmesan cheeses until the cheeses have melted and the soup is thick. Stir in the pureed broccoli. Let the soup cool, transfer it to a bowl, cover it, and refrigerate it. You can make this soup up to 3 days in advance. When you're ready to serve, gently reheat the soup on low until it's warmed through, transfer it to bowls or shot glasses, and garnish it with the dill.

Smoked Salmon with Hard-Cooked Eggs, Red Onion, and Crème Fraîche

Allow 2 to 3 ounces per person

Buy the very best smoked salmon you can afford, or make your own Gravlax, page 40, garnish it with the suggestions in the recipe title, and as shown at left, and serve.

Stone-Crab Claws with Best-Ever Mustard Sauce for Seafood

Allow 2 crabs per person

Best-quality stone-crab claws—Joe's Stone Crab is a good
   source
Best-Ever Mustard Sauce, recipe follows

BEST-EVER MUSTARD SAUCE
Makes 2¼ cups, enough for 20 to 30 crab claws

1½ teaspoons saffron threads, softened in 1 cup warm
   chicken stock, and drained
1 Cup Perfect Homemade Mayonnaise, page 28,
   or Hellmann's
1 cup sour cream
¼ cup Dijon mustard
2 tablespoons freshly squeezed lemon juice
1½ teaspoons salt
¼ teaspoon freshly ground black pepper

Combine all the ingredients in a mixing bowl and stir them well to combine. Refrigerate the sauce in an airtight container for at least 4 hours and up to 7 days. Serve the sauce cold along side the stone crabs, or any old cold seafood you like, for that matter.

This fern pattern from William Yeoward is another of my very favorite things—see page 17.

Standing Rib Roast with Horseradish Sauce and Yorkshire Pudding

Serves 10 to 12

1 (8-pound) standing beef rib roast
4 teaspoons salt
2 teaspoons ground black pepper
¼ cup minced garlic
2 tablespoons dried thyme
2 cups red wine
1 cup beef stock
Horseradish Sauce, for serving, recipe follows
Yorkshire Pudding, for serving, recipe follows

Preheat the oven to 450°F.

Place the roast in a large bowl and toss it with the salt, pepper, and garlic until it is fully covered on all sides with the seasonings and garlic. Place the seasoned roast in a roasting pan, making sure to scrape all of the seasonings from the bowl onto the roast. Pour the wine and stock over it, and place it in the oven uncovered.

Let it roast for 20 minutes exactly, then reduce the temperature to 350°F for another 1¾ hours. Remove the roast from the oven and let it rest for 30 minutes before carving and serving. The resting is the most important step, so make sure it's fully rested for 30 minutes exactly!

HORSERADISH SAUCE
Makes 1¾ cups

½ cup prepared horseradish, well drained
1 cup sour cream
½ cup Perfect Homemade Mayonnaise, page 28
    or Hellman's
2 tablespoons freshly squeezed lemon juice
1 teaspoon Dijon mustard
¾ teaspoon salt
⅛ teaspoon cayenne pepper
⅛ teaspoon ground white pepper

In a small bowl, combine all the ingredients, stirring them until they are well combined. Cover the bowl, refrigerate the sauce overnight, and serve.

YORKSHIRE PUDDING
Makes 24 popovers

8 tablespoons (1 stick) butter, melted
6 eggs, at room temperature
5¼ cups milk
1¾ teaspoons salt
¾ teaspoon ground black pepper
½ teaspoon ground nutmeg
3 cups all-purpose flour

Note: You will need 2 Popover Pans with 12 half-cup openings.

Preheat the oven to 425°F. Place the popover pans on 2 heavy baking sheets. Brush the popover pans with the melted butter (about 1 teaspoon per cup) and place them in the preheated oven for 10 minutes. Place the eggs in a large bowl and lightly beat them.

Combine the milk, salt, pepper, and nutmeg in a large heavy saucepan over medium heat. Heat the milk mixture until it's scalding but not boiling. Gradually pour the hot milk mixture into the eggs, whisking vigorously until all of the milk and eggs are combined. Place the flour in a sieve or sifter, and sift it over the egg-milk mixture. Whisk the mixture until it just comes together to make a batter, being careful to avoid overbeating.

Pour the batter into measuring cups so that it can be easily poured into the hot pans. Working quickly, remove the baking sheets and popover pans from the oven and completely fill each of the heated cups (the cups should be filled to the brim). Return the baking sheets and popover pans to the oven, and bake them for 10 minutes. After 10 minutes, decrease the temperature to 375°F, and continue to bake the popovers for an additional 25 minutes, until they are crusty and brown on the outside. Turn the oven off, and let the popovers rest in the oven for another 10 minutes.

Remove the popovers from the oven and let them rest for a couple of minutes before serving them, or let them cool for up to 8 hours, before reheating them and serving them later.

Fettucine with Black Truffles and Parmesan

Serves 10 to 12

1 quart heavy cream
1¼ teaspoons salt
1 teaspoon ground black pepper
1 tablespoon minced garlic
½ teaspoon grated nutmeg
2 cups grated Parmesan cheese
1 pound fettucine, cooked in salted water until
    al dente, drained but still warm
1 ounce fresh black truffles, shaved very thinly—don't
    hesitate to add more if your budget allows!
Shaved Parmesan cheese, for garnish

In a large heavy saucepan over medium-low heat, combine the cream, salt, pepper, garlic, and nutmeg. Let the mixture steep for 30 minutes before turning up the heat to bring it to a boil. Once the mixture comes to a boil, immediately reduce the heat and vigorously whisk in the grated Parmesan cheese, a little at a time, until it is fully combined and the sauce is smooth and thick. Pour the hot sauce over the drained pasta, toss it well, and serve it in a warmed bowl. Top with the shaved truffles and shaved Parmesan cheese.

Sliced Ibérico Ham

Allow 1 to 2 ounces per person

Another one that's fairly self-explanatory . . . and the ultimate crowd-pleaser. This is a show-stopper, and it's always good to have a bit of theatre at your parties.

Avocado, Orange, Grapefruit, and Red Onion Salad with Arugula and Macadamia Nuts

Makes 10 to 12 servings

2 large navel oranges, peeled, and sectioned
1 large Texas ruby red grapefruit, peeled, and sectioned
3 tablespoons roasted whole macadamia nuts
½ red onion, finely diced
1 firmly packed cup arugula
1 large avocado, cut into large chunks
½ teaspoon salt
¼ teaspoon ground black pepper
½ cup Poppy Seed Vinaigrette, recipe follows

In a large bowl combine the oranges, grapefruit, macadamia nuts, and onions. Just before serving, to avoid browning, peel the avocado, slice it into large chunks, and add the chunks to the bowl. Add the vinaigrette and toss the salad at least sixteen times, trying to avoid breaking up the avocado.

POPPY SEED VINAIGRETTE
Makes 4 cups

1 cup red wine vinegar
3 tablespoons poppy seeds
3 tablespoons minced red onion
3 tablespoons minced garlic
2 tablespoons dry mustard
1 tablespoon salt
½ cup sugar
1 teaspoon ground black pepper
3 cups vegetable oil

In a medium mixing bowl whisk together all the ingredients except for the vegetable oil. Add the vegetable oil slowly in droplets, whisking constantly to make the perfect emulsion.

Note: This makes more than you will need for the salad but keep it in your refrigerator—it will disappear!

Strawberry Pots-de-Crème with Red Fruit Coulis

Makes 8 servings

1 pound strawberries, stemmed
8 large egg yolks
¾ cup superfine sugar
¼ teaspoon salt
2½ cups heavy cream
3 tablespoons Chambord
Red Fruit Coulis, recipe follows

Preheat the oven to 275°F. In the bowl of a food processor fitted with a metal blade, process the strawberries, egg yolks, sugar, and salt until the mixture is very smooth.

Strain the mixture through a fine sieve into a medium bowl. Add the cream and Chambord, and stir the mixture with a wooden spoon or a rubber spatula until it is fully combined. Divide the mixture evenly among eight 1-cup ramekins. Bring a kettle of water to a boil on the stove. Place the ramekins in a deep baking dish, and add enough boiling water to come halfway up the sides of the ramekins.

Place the baking dish in the oven and bake until the custard is just set, about 1 hour. Remove the dish from the oven, and place the ramekins on a cooling rack. Once they are completely cool, cover them and refrigerate for at least 6 hours and up to 4 days before serving.

Serve the Pots-de-Crème garnished with the Red Fruit Coulis.

RED FRUIT COULIS

½ cup fresh or frozen strawberries, stemmed if fresh
½ cup fresh or frozen raspberries
¼ cup superfine sugar
2 tablespoons Chambord

Combine the ingredients in the bowl of a food processor fitted with the metal blade and process them until they are smooth. You can make and refrigerate the coulis up to 4 days in advance.

Butterscotch White-Chocolate Pecan Cookies

Makes 50 to 60 small cookies

½ pound (2 sticks) butter
1½ cups firmly packed light brown sugar
1 large egg
1 tablespoon pure vanilla extract
1¾ cups all-purpose flour
1 teaspoon salt
½ teaspoon baking powder
½ teaspoon baking soda
1 cup butterscotch chips
¾ cup white chocolate chips
1¼ cups toasted pecans, coarsely chopped

In the bowl of an electric stand mixer fitted with the paddle attachment, cream the butter and sugar together on medium-high speed until the mixture is light and fluffy, about 5 minutes. Turn the mixer to low, add the egg, and then the vanilla, continuing to mix until everything is well blended. Turn the mixer off.

In a mixing bowl, whisk together the flour, salt, baking powder, and baking soda. Turn the mixer to the lowest speed and add the flour mixture, gradually in batches, to the butter-sugar mixture, being extremely careful not to mix the dough too much. Fold in the butterscotch and white chocolate chips, and the chopped pecans by hand, and refrigerate the dough in its bowl for half an hour.

Preheat the oven to 350°F. Line a heavy baking sheet with parchment paper and, using a half-ounce scoop to portion the dough, place balls of dough onto the prepared baking sheet in rows of five. Bake them for 5 minutes before turning the pan and baking them for 3 to 5 minutes more, until they are just done. As with every single cookie under the sun, the more you underbake them, the better they are.

Coconut-Raspberry Rum Cake

Makes 16 servings

FOR THE CAKE:
6 tablespoons cold butter
8 tablespoons (1 stick) butter, melted
2¼ cups granulated sugar
1½ tablespoons pure vanilla extract
5 egg yolks, plus 3 whole eggs
2½ cups cake flour
1 tablespoon salt
1 tablespoon baking powder
½ cup buttermilk
¾ cup heavy cream

FOR THE GLAZE:
½ cup coconut milk
½ cup light rum
2 tablespoons confectioners' sugar

FOR THE ICING:
18 ounces cream cheese, at room temperature
½ pound (2 sticks) plus 2 tablespoons butter,
    at room temperature
3 tablespoons clear vanilla extract
7½ cups confectioners' sugar
2¼ teaspoons salt
6 tablespoons coconut milk
1 package (5⅓ cups) sweetened flaked coconut
1½ cups seedless raspberry jam
1½ cups fresh shaved coconut, firmly packed, for garnish
Fresh raspberries, for garnish

TO MAKE THE CAKE:
Preheat the oven to 325°F. In the bowl of an electric stand mixer fitted with the paddle attachment, beat the cold butter until it's very light, about 5 minutes, scraping down the bowl several times during the beating. Gradually add the granulated sugar. While continuing to beat, add the vanilla, and beat the mixture for 5 more minutes, scraping the bowl again. The mixture will be very coarse. Add the melted butter to the mixture at lowest speed, and then the egg yolks, and whole eggs, still mixing on very low speed. Turn off the mixer.

In a large bowl, sift together the flour, salt, and baking powder. In another bowl, mix the buttermilk and cream together. Turn the mixer on to the lowest speed, and add half of the flour and then half of the buttermilk-cream mixtures. Then add the remaining flour mixture and the remaining buttermilk-cream mixture. Scrape down the bowl as necessary. Do not overmix this batter or the cake will be tough.

Butter and flour three 9-inch cake pans, put a parchment round in the bottom of the pans, and butter and flour the rounds. Pour equal portions of the batter into the three prepared pans, tap each pan on a sturdy surface to release the air bubbles, if there are any, and bake them for 25 to 30 minutes, until the cakes' color is a brown that's a little darker than golden and a toothpick or knife comes out clean. Cool the cakes for 10 minutes, then run a knife around the edges, and invert the cakes onto a cold baking sheet.

TO MAKE THE GLAZE:
In a mixing bowl, whisk together the coconut milk, rum, and confectioners' sugar.

TO MAKE THE ICING:
In the bowl of an electric stand mixer fitted with the paddle attachment, combine the cream cheese, butter, and vanilla extract, and beat them on medium speed until they're light and fluffy, about 5 minutes.

In a large mixing bowl, combine the confectioners' sugar and salt, and add it to the cream cheese mixture, one cup at a time, beating on medium speed after each addition, until it is smooth. Turn the mixer to the lowest speed, and stir in the coconut milk and sweetened flaked coconut.

TO ASSEMBLE THE CAKE:
When you're ready to ice the cake, slice each layer horizontally in half so that you have 6 layers. They must be completely cool before you start to assemble the cake. Place the layers one by one on a cake stand. Pierce each layer with a fork in several places and then spoon or brush the glaze over each layer before icing it. Add the raspberry jam to alternating layers, and spread it evenly. Ice each layer, using approximately 1 cup of icing per layer, and then garnish the finished cake with the fresh coconut shavings and fresh raspberries.

THE GRAMMYS, OSCARS, STEEPLECHASE, OR THE BIG GAME

COLD SWEET POTATO, COCONUT,
AND CORIANDER SOUP

SPINACH AND ARTICHOKE DIP WITH
CRUDITÉS AND TOASTED PITA

PERFECT GUACAMOLE WITH
BLUE CORN CHIPS

PRALINE BACON

OVEN "FRIED" CHICKEN

VELVET EGG SALAD
OPEN-FACED SANDWICHES

ASPARAGUS SPEARS
WITH PROSCIUTTO

MARINATED SHRIMP SALAD

BEST-EVER BROWNIES WITH SALTED
CARAMEL, WALNUTS, AND BOURBON

STRAWBERRIES ROMANOFF

PERFECT PEANUT BUTTER COOKIES

hen I first started to live in Los Angeles more than twenty years ago, no one there knew much at all about basic Southern food—but if there's a complicated food fad of the moment, Angelenos embrace it. Or they eat the odd lettuce leaf every other Tuesday, drink some coconut water, work out, and call it a day.

During the week of the Oscars in L.A., the streets shut down. The businesses close early. Extra cops are brought in to direct traffic. Even the trees seem different. As for the parties, it's a tsunami of hobnobbing, and it's big business. I inherited an annual party from San Francisco socialite Denise Hale, who'd had pre-eminent Hollywood days as the second wife of fabled golden-age director Vincente Minnelli—father to Liza—from his marriage to first wife Judy Garland. Denise's party—then mine— was the Saturday night before the Oscars, a dinner she'd hosted for more than forty years by the time she gave it to me. After her dinner at Spago in 2003 she said, "Okay, darling. Now this is your night."

My first dinner for the Oscars was in February 2004, an event I hosted for more than a decade starting as a dinner for twelve—with Denise in attendance—swelling to a dinner of almost two hundred, and then going back much more reasonably ten years later to around forty—with Denise still in attendance. I always served the simplest of Southern staples—a soul-pleasing menu much like this one—and was gratified years later to find many posh Hollywood hosts serving fried chicken, corn pudding, and salted caramel cake at tony Oscar events around town. Like almost everything else in this book, do it all ahead and become a guest at your own party. You deserve it.

Denise Hale at the party she "gave" to me at my house in Los Angeles, February, 2010.

Cold Sweet Potato, Coconut, and Coriander Soup

Makes 10 to 12 servings

4 tablespoons (½ stick) butter
4 tablespoons olive oil
2 pounds sweet potatoes, cut into ½- to ¾-inch cubes
4 leeks, the white parts only, chopped
2 teaspoons coriander seeds
4 tablespoons finely chopped fresh cilantro, divided
4½ cups chicken stock
2 (13½-ounce) cans coconut milk
1½ teaspoons salt
¼ teaspoon ground white pepper

Melt the butter and olive oil together in a Dutch oven over a medium-low heat. When the foaming has subsided, add the sweet potato, leeks, coriander seeds, and half of the chopped cilantro. Let the vegetables steep with a lid on until the leeks are tender and translucent, 15 to 20 minutes. Stir the pot occasionally to prevent the sweet potato from sticking.

Add the stock, 2¼ cups of the coconut milk, the salt, and pepper, and let it simmer for another 15 minutes until the sweet potato is tender. Remove the pot from the heat, add the remaining coconut milk, and puree the soup, in batches, in a food processor fitted with the metal blade or with an immersion blender. Pour the soup into a tureen, or soup bowls, and garnish it with the remaining cilantro.

Spinach and Artichoke Dip with Crudités and Toasted Pita

Makes 6 cups, enough for 20 to 30 servings

Perfect Creamed Spinach, page 48
2 (14-ounce) cans artichoke hearts, packed in water, drained
1 large onion, chopped
1 cup Perfect Homemade Mayonnaise, page 28, or Hellman's
1 cup sour cream
1½ cups shredded mozzarella cheese, firmly packed
¼ teaspoon salt
½ teaspoon cracked black pepper

Preheat the oven to 350°F. Butter a 9 by 13-inch baking dish.

Place the Perfect Creamed Spinach in a large mixing bowl. In a food processor fitted with a metal blade, process the artichoke hearts and onion until they are fully chopped but still chunky. Add them to the mixing bowl with the creamed spinach and stir in the mayonnaise, sour cream, mozzarella, and salt. Transfer the mixture to the prepared baking dish. Top it with the black pepper and bake it for about 25 minutes, until the dip is golden brown and bubbly.

Perfect Guacamole with Blue Corn Chips

Makes 4 cups, enough for 10 to 12 servings

3 large or 6 small ripe avocados
1 cup chopped red onion
½ cup chopped fresh cilantro
2 tablespoons freshly squeezed lemon juice
1½ teaspoons salt
¾ teaspoon freshly ground black pepper
Blue corn chips, for serving

Combine the avocados, onion, cilantro, lemon juice, salt, and pepper in a food processor fitted with the metal blade. Pulse them until they are combined but still chunky. Transfer the guacamole to a serving bowl and serve it immediately with the blue corn chips.

Praline Bacon

Makes about 50 small hors d'oeuvres

1 pound thick-cut bacon
¾ cup firmly packed dark brown sugar
¼ cup granulated sugar
¼ teaspoon salt
1 cup pecan halves

Preheat the oven to 350°F. Line a baking sheet with aluminum foil. Arrange the bacon in a single layer on the prepared baking sheet. Bake it until the bacon browns and the fat is rendered and bubbly, but the bacon is not completely cooked, about 30 minutes.

Meanwhile, combine both sugars, the salt, and pecans in the bowl of a food processor fitted with a metal blade. Process the mixture until the pecans are finely chopped. Add the mixture to a large mixing bowl.

Remove the bacon from the oven but keep the oven on. Add the bacon to the bowl with the pecan mixture, and pat it down so that the sugar-pecan mixture fully covers the bacon. Return the coated bacon to the baking sheet, and bake it until the bacon is crisp, about 10 more minutes. Cool the bacon on the rack for at least 30 minutes before cutting the bacon into bite-size pieces and serving. These hors d'oeuvres can be prepared up to 3 days in advance. Keep the bite-size pieces in an airtight container in the refrigerator. Bring them to room temperature before serving.

Oven "Fried" Chicken

Makes 10 pieces, enough for 4 to 6 servings

1 (4- to 5-pound) "fryer" chicken, cut into 10 pieces—the
    breasts should be cut in half
4 teaspoons salt, divided
2 teaspoons ground black pepper, divided
1 cup all-purpose flour
1½ teaspoons dried oregano
¼ teaspoon cayenne pepper
1 cup plus 4 tablespoons clarified butter
½ lemon, cut into 4 wedges

Preheat the oven to 375°F. Rinse and thoroughly dry
the chicken pieces.

In a large mixing bowl, toss the chicken pieces with
2 teaspoons of the salt and 1 teaspoon of the ground
black pepper until the chicken has absorbed the spices
and there is nothing left in the bowl.

In a small mixing bowl whisk together the flour,
1½ teaspoons of the salt, the remaining teaspoon black
pepper, the oregano, and cayenne pepper. Add the flour
mixture to the seasoned chicken, and toss it thoroughly
until the pieces are well coated, 25 to 30 times. There

will be some flour mixture that is not absorbed by
the chicken; reserve it.

Heat 1 cup of the clarified butter with the remaining
½ teaspoon salt in a large heavy skillet over medium-
high heat. When it starts to bubble, add the chicken
pieces to the pan one by one, skin side down. Sprinkle
the top side of the chicken with the leftover flour
mixture. After about 5 minutes, when the skin side is
golden brown, turn the chicken pieces over, and add
the remaining ¼ cup clarified butter to the pan. Let
the chicken sear an additional 4 to 5 minutes, until it is
browned on all sides.

Transfer the uncovered skillet to the preheated oven and
bake it for 25 to 30 minutes, until the chicken is fully
brown and tender and the juices run clear when pierced
with a knife—although I really recommend you do not
pierce the chicken with a knife because all of the fantastic
juices run out if you do. Remove the chicken from the
oven, and transfer the pieces to a serving platter. Spoon
the cracklings from the pan over the chicken. Squeeze the
lemon wedges over the hot chicken, and let the chicken
rest for at least 10 minutes before serving. This chicken
can also be served room temperature or cold.

The Oscar Party: Dinner for 150 at
home in Los Angeles, February 2011.

Velvet Egg Salad Open-Faced Sandwiches

Makes 2 pounds, enough for 20 small sandwiches

30 hard-boiled eggs, peeled, the whites removed, and discarded
1½ cups Perfect Homemade Mayonnaise, page 28, or Hellman's
1 large shallot, minced
1 teaspoon salt
¼ teaspoon freshly ground white pepper
¾ pound Gruyère cheese, grated
1 tablespoon grated Parmesan cheese
1 tablespoon plus 1 teaspoon dried dill

In the bowl of a food processor fitted with the metal blade, place the egg yolks, mayonnaise, shallot, salt, pepper, cheeses, and dill and process until smooth (somewhat chunkier is okay, too; it's your preference). Transfer the salad to a bowl, cover it with foil or plastic wrap, and refrigerate it at least 8 hours and up to 3 days before serving.

When you're ready to serve, spread the mixture on one side of whatever bread you like, and use a biscuit cutter to create perfectly sized open-faced sandwiches.

Asparagus Spears with Prosciutto

Makes 12 to 16 servings

24 asparagus spears, blanched in salted water and cooled
24 slices of prosciutto

Wrap the slices of prosciutto around the asparagus and serve.

Marinated Shrimp Salad

Makes 12 to 15 servings

3 tablespoons butter
2½ pounds shrimp (26–30 count), peeled and deveined
1 cup vegetable oil
¾ cup Perfect Homemade Mayonnaise, page 28, or Hellman's
¼ cup apple cider vinegar
1 cup diced onion
2 teaspoons salt
¾ teaspoon ground white pepper
2¼ teaspoons dried dill

Melt the butter in a large heavy skillet over medium heat. Add the shrimp and sauté them until they are just cooked through, approximately 5 minutes. Remove them from the skillet, drain them in a colander, and let them cool for at least thirty minutes.

In a large bowl, combine the oil, vinegar, onion, salt, white pepper, and dill. Add the shrimp and mix, then refrigerate, covered, for at least 6 hours or overnight. Serve cold.

Best-Ever Brownies with Salted Caramel, Walnuts, and Bourbon

Makes 28 to 32 small brownies

FOR THE BROWNIES:
8 ounces unsweetened chocolate
¾ pound (3 sticks) butter
4 cups sugar
6 eggs
1 tablespoon vanilla extract
1 tablespoon plus 1 pinch of salt
2 cups all-purpose flour

FOR THE GLAZE:
1 tablespoon butter
½ pound light brown sugar
1 egg yolk
½ cup heavy cream
½ teaspoon salt
2 teaspoons vanilla extract
2 tablespoons excellent-quality bourbon
¾ cup chopped walnuts

Preheat the oven to 350°F. Butter a 9 by 13-inch metal baking pan.

TO MAKE THE BROWNIES:
In a double boiler over low heat, melt the chocolate and the butter together. Place the melted chocolate and butter mixture in a large mixing bowl and stir in the sugar until it is well combined. Add the eggs, vanilla extract, and salt and stir until they are just combined. Fold in the flour.

Note: Be sure to mix these by hand, and not too much, as their texture will be gooier and fudgier the less uniform the batter is.

Pour the mixture into the prepared baking pan and bake the brownies for 32 to 35 minutes. Do not overbake them. They should be set but still move a tiny bit when the pan is shaken, and most seasoned brownie chefs would say that they are not quite done. They will be very soft, and very difficult to handle, but completely worth it. Let the brownies cool for 1 hour, uncovered.

TO MAKE THE GLAZE:
In a heavy saucepan or a double boiler over low heat, melt the butter, brown sugar, egg yolk, heavy cream, and salt and stir them together until the sugar has dissolved. Be careful not to burn the sugar. Remove the saucepan from the heat, and stir in the vanilla and bourbon.

Once the brownies have cooled, pierce them with a fork every ¼ to ½ inch, and pour half of the glaze over the brownies. It will soak in. Spread the walnuts in an even layer on the brownies and top them with the remaining glaze. Freeze the brownies to make them easy to cut, then cut them, and serve them warm with vanilla ice cream or on their own at room temperature. There is no way to go wrong here.

Strawberries Romanoff

Makes 16 to 20 servings

2½ cups sour cream
½ cup firmly packed brown sugar
3 tablespoons brandy
¼ teaspoon salt
1 pint fresh strawberries, washed and dried

Combine the sour cream, brown sugar, brandy, and salt in a bowl, and whisk them together until they are well combined and the sugar has dissolved. Serve the sauce alongside the fresh strawberries.

Perfect Peanut Butter Cookies

Makes 50 cookies

10 tablespoons butter
1 cup peanut butter
2 cups firmly packed dark brown sugar
1 teaspoon salt
2 tablespoons plus ¼ teaspoon vanilla
1 cup all-purpose flour

Preheat the oven to 375°F. In the bowl of an electric stand mixer fitted with the paddle attachment, cream the butter, peanut butter, brown sugar, and salt on medium speed until they are combined, approximately 3 minutes. Add the vanilla, and then the flour, a little at a time, until it's just combined—do not overmix. Transfer the dough to plastic wrap to cover it, and set it in the refrigerator for 30 minutes.

Assemble a 9 by 13-inch baking sheet with parchment paper. Portion the dough with a half-ounce scoop and drop the balls of dough, evenly spaced, onto the prepared baking sheet. Bake the cookies for 8 to 10 minutes, until they are just done and have spread a small bit. Like most other cookies under the sun, underbaking is the secret to making them sensational. Let them cool before serving.

VALENTINE'S DAY OF AN UTMOST APHRODISIAC SORT

AUNT LAURA'S SCALLOPED OYSTERS

STEAK AU POIVRE

WATERCRESS AND
ENDIVE SALAD WITH ROQUEFORT

CHOCOLATE-DIPPED STRAWBERRIES

Succulent, sexy, easy, elegant—these are but four words to capture the indescribable feeling of sophistication and accomplishment making a really good steak au poivre can—straight from the skillet to your gorgeous finished plate in mere minutes. This menu is so chic that it's sure to impress that special whomever with your incredible culinary acumen, your immense sense of style, and your worldly continental élan. How's that for openers?

"Tableside" preparation in elegant restaurants, ubiquitous in a period we now refer to as "mid-century" has gone drastically out of fashion. Now we've got elaborately plated dinners that resemble specimens from the science fair, with foams and test tubes that arrive on black square plates curling up at their edges. Let's just say that it's not so often you see dishes like steak au poivre, caesar salad, steak tartare, crêpes suzette, and bananas foster prepared tableside, all of which were deliciously impressive events that flamed up on a night-ly basis in America's finest dining establishments. Why not? These dishes, prepared just for you, are theatre. They are delicious. They are WOW. You're OUT for dinner, and this is one special occasion.

But tonight, you're IN for dinner, and, yes, this is still one special occasion. Set your table ahead of time and make it pretty. Pour a glass of wine. Light the candles, and then . . . crush those peppercorns! It's easy and fun, and you'll be able to release a few endorphins. A promise of more to come.

A fantastic way to start the whole thing is with some Champagne and Aunt Laura's Scalloped Oysters. My mother's younger sister was a sweetheart—ebullient, vivacious, and fun. She was an accomplished horsewoman, a lover of gardens, houses, houndstooth checks, bouclé plaids, orchids, red convertibles, standard poodles, parties, gossip, black coffee, Chardonnay, and Marlboro Red cigarettes. I miss her. Let's just say she saw the irony in things. She was proudly not a cook, and had better things to do than languish in the kitchen, but Aunt Laura appreciated delicious food and mastered a few key dishes—her scalloped oysters being my very favorite of all of them.

ABOVE: *Aunt Laura catching my mother's wedding bouquet as "Devotedly, Betty" looks on, Piedmont Driving Club, Atlanta, December 1964.* RIGHT: *Chocolate-Dipped Strawberries, page 136.*

Aunt Laura's Scalloped Oysters

Makes 10 to 12 servings, more than enough for this menu but you will love having these left over

FOR THE VEGETABLES:
4 tablespoons (½ stick) butter
½ white onion, diced
2 large shallots, minced
½ pound sliced mushrooms
1 teaspoon minced garlic
¼ teaspoon salt
¼ teaspoon ground black pepper
3 tablespoons sherry

FOR THE SAUCE:
1½ cups heavy cream
½ cup milk
1 teaspoon minced garlic
1½ teaspoons salt
⅛ teaspoon freshly ground white pepper
¼ teaspoon plus ⅛ teaspoon freshly ground
   black pepper
¼ teaspoon freshly grated nutmeg
½ cup bourbon
5 tablespoons freshly squeezed lemon juice
2 teaspoons chicken stock base
6 tablespoons (¾ stick) butter
4 tablespoons all-purpose flour
1 cup grated Parmesan cheese
1 cup fresh chives, chopped

FOR THE OYSTERS:
6 tablespoons (¾ stick) butter, melted
3 cups fresh plain white breadcrumbs
48 ounces of shucked oysters, thoroughly drained

Preheat the oven to 425°F. Butter a 9 by 13-inch baking dish.

TO SAUTÉ THE VEGETABLES:
Melt the butter in a heavy skillet over medium-high heat. When the foaming has subsided, add the onions and shallots, and sauté them until they are translucent, but not colored, about 5 to 7 minutes. Add the mushrooms,

garlic, salt, and black pepper, and continue to sauté them until the mushrooms begin to soften, about 4 minutes. Add the sherry, and sauté for another 4 minutes, until the vegetables are soft but not mushy. Remove the pan from the heat and set it aside.

TO MAKE THE SAUCE:
In a heavy saucepan over medium heat, combine the cream, milk, garlic, salt, white pepper, black pepper, nutmeg, bourbon, lemon juice, and chicken stock base and and whisk them together. Bring the mixture to a scalding temperature but do not boil it. In a heavy skillet over medium heat, melt the butter, and add the flour to make a roux. Stir it with a wooden spoon or a rubber spatula until it is fully cooked through but not brown, about 3 to 4 minutes. Add the roux to the scalding milk-cream mixture, and whisk it thoroughly to get the lumps out. Turn up the heat, and bring the mixture to a boil to thicken the sauce. When it boils, it will be as thick as it will ever be without reducing it. Turn off the heat, and whisk in the Parmesan cheese, then add the chives and cooked vegetables. Stir the sauce well to combine. Remove the mixture from the stove, and set it aside.

TO ASSEMBLE THE DISH:
In a small mixing bowl, combine the melted butter with the breadcrumbs. Spread 1½ cups of the buttered breadcrumbs evenly in the bottom of the prepared baking dish. Place the baking dish in the oven for 3 to 4 minutes to toast the breadcrumbs. Remove the baking dish from the oven.

Place the drained oysters on top of the toasted bread-crumbs. Using a rubber spatula, spread the sauce evenly over the oysters. The dish can be prepared to this point, covered, and refrigerated for up to 2 days before bringing it to room temperature again for final baking. Top the casserole with the remaining 1½ cups buttered bread-crumbs. Bake the scalloped oysters in the oven for 15 to 18 minutes, until the breadcrumbs are golden brown, and the oysters and sauce are bubbling. Remove the dish from the oven, and let it cool for 5 minutes before serving.

Steak au Poivre

Makes 4 servings

1 tablespoon mixed peppercorns
1 (1-pound) filet mignon, cut into 4 (4-ounce) steaks
¼ teaspoon salt
⅛ teaspoon freshly ground black pepper
2 tablespoons butter
1 tablespoon tasteless vegetable oil
2 tablespoon Dijon mustard
4 tablespoons cognac or brandy
4 tablespoons heavy cream

Layer one zip-top bag inside another, pour in the peppercorns, and pound them with a meat tenderizer or rolling pin until they are coarsely crushed.

Place the steaks, salt, and pepper in a bowl, and toss them until the steaks are fully seasoned on all sides.

In a large heavy skillet over high heat, heat the butter and oil. When the foaming of the butter has subsided, add the steaks and sauté them for 1½ minutes per side for perfect medium-rare. Remove the steaks to a serving platter and add the crushed peppercorns, mustard, cognac, and cream to the skillet, cooking them for another minute or two until they come together to form a sauce, and, using a spatula, release the bits stuck to the pan.

Pour the sauce over the steaks and serve them immediately.

Watercress and Endive Salad with Roquefort

Makes 6 servings

4 cups loosely packed watercress
4 heads Belgian endive, sliced
3 ounces Roquefort cheese, crumbled
½ cup chopped toasted walnuts
½ teaspoon salt
¼ teaspoon freshly ground black pepper
The Easiest, Best Vinaigrette in the World, page 28

Add all ingredients to a large mixing bowl, and toss them at least 40 times. Serve the salad cold, and don't ever be afraid to do it ahead, as the soggier the greens get, and the longer they have to marinate, the better the flavors will be.

Chocolate-Dipped Strawberries

Makes 12 to 14 strawberries

12 to 14 strawberries (about ½ pound), washed and dried
3 ounces dark chocolate

Assemble a 9 by 13-inch metal baking sheet with parchment paper. Over medium-low heat in a double boiler, melt the chocolate until it's completely smooth. Remove the chocolate from the heat, and dip the strawberries in the chocolate, covering as much of them or as little as you like. Place the chocolate-dipped strawberries on the parchment paper, and place the sheet in the refrigerator until the chocolate has cooled and hardened before serving. They will set fairly quickly, but you can serve these up to 3 days after dipping them in the melted chocolate.

Vivacious and fun Aunt Laura (left), in my grandmother's living room, Atlanta, 1963.

After a good dinner one can forgive anybody, even one's own relations.
—Oscar Wilde

AN EASY SUNDAY SUPPER TO IMPRESS EVEN YOUR IN-LAWS

SENSATIONAL SMASHED POTATOES

ROASTED CHERRY TOMATOES

BUTTER LETTUCE SALAD WITH CHIVES AND HERBS, PAGE 32

GUARANTEED: THE PERFECT ROAST CHICKEN

HONEY BEAR'S—AND—POLLY'S MIXED BERRY CRUMBLE WITH PERFECT FRENCH VANILLA ICE CREAM

If a good cook is measured by his ability to properly roast a chicken, then I am afraid to do the math on how many less than properly-abled cooks there are. But for this menu, I wanted to share what I think is the very best roast chicken ever, so easy to do that the only skill you'll need is being able to read. Cook with confidence and serve it forth—I won't let you down.

As for the dessert crumble, this recipe is inspired by Polly and Honey Bear—the fantastic daughters-in-law of my dear late friend Betsy Bloomingdale, perhaps most widely now known as the best friend to Nancy Reagan. Betsy was a superb hostess, great foodie, and a grand and stylish lady who lavishly entertained the gratin of Holly-

wood, the government, and the international beau monde, at lunches and dinners for more than sixty years. Betsy had the most marvelous mid-century neoclassical house in Holmby Hills, L.A., she'd designed with husband, Alfred, who, among other things, invented the credit card, and with Holly-wood star turned decorator Billy Haines. The house is a masterpiece, certainly the best example of the Hollywood Regency style ever, and is now owned by fashion designer Tom Ford. Betsy marveled at the intelligence and abilities of her daughters-in-law, and was singularly proud of being an only child who'd brought forth three great children, eight grandchildren, and, by the time she died, four great-grandchildren—all the while perfectly coiffed and tucked, and looking like never less than a proper star from the studio system's golden age. Betsy was cozy, fun, and amusing, and a delight to be with, always—and, like so many strong, stylish women, knew exactly what she liked and didn't, without equivocation. She put me wise to this delicious crumble long before I ever had it, and with just one bite I was sold. I promise—if it met Betsy's approval, you'll hit a home run, bases loaded, with your family.

ABOVE: *Betsy Bloomingdale in her Holmby Hills atrium, Los Angeles, 1958.* RIGHT: *Sensational Smashed Potatoes, page 142.*

Sensational Smashed Potatoes

Makes 6 servings

3 teaspoons salt, divided
2 pounds medium (size B) Yukon Gold potatoes
½ teaspoon ground black pepper
½ teaspoon cracked black pepper
½ cup olive oil
Sour cream, crumbled bacon, Cheddar cheese, and chives, or crème fraiche, smoked salmon bits, and caviar, for garnish

Bring 2 quarts water and 2 teaspoons of the salt to a boil in a 6-quart stockpot over high heat. Add the potatoes and boil them for 20 to 25 minutes, until they are tender and fully cooked through.

Preheat the oven to 425°F. Drain the potatoes in a colander. Place them on a heavy baking sheet. Using the bottom of a 9 by 13-inch glass baking dish, flat spatula, or a fork, smash the potatoes down to a height of ¾ inch, and season them on both sides with the remaining teaspoon salt, the ground black pepper, and the cracked black pepper. Pour the olive oil over the potatoes and place the baking sheet in the oven for 35 to 40 minutes, until the potatoes are brown and crisp.

Remove the potatoes from the oven and let them rest for at least 5 minutes before assembling them on a serving platter. Garnish them with any of the choices above or some option that I haven't thought of yet, and serve.

Roasted Cherry Tomatoes

Makes 4 to 6 servings

2 pints cherry tomatoes
¼ cup olive oil
¼ teaspoon salt
⅛ teaspoon ground black pepper

Preheat the oven to 400°F.

In a medium bowl combine the tomatoes, olive oil, salt, and pepper, and toss them thoroughly. Spread the tomatoes on a large baking sheet, and roast them in the oven for 20 minutes until they have blistered a bit. Let the roasted tomatoes cool to room temperature, about 10 minutes, before serving.

Guaranteed: The Perfect Roast Chicken

Makes 4 to 6 servings

8 tablespoons (1 stick) butter, at room temperature
2 cloves garlic, minced, plus 1 whole clove
1 (4-pound) roasting chicken, at room temperature,
    the cavity emptied
2 teaspoons salt
1 teaspoon ground black pepper
1½ teaspoons dried tarragon
1 lemon, cut in half and deseeded
1 cup dry white wine

Preheat the oven to 450°F. In a small mixing bowl, mash together the butter and two-thirds of the garlic with a fork to make a compound butter.

In a large mixing bowl, toss together the chicken, salt, pepper, and tarragon until the chicken is fully coated on all sides with the seasonings. Place the seasoned chicken in a metal roasting pan, making certain to gather any excess seasonings from the mixing bowl. Squeeze both halves of the lemon over the chicken, and put the squeezed lemons inside the cavity with the remaining minced garlic. Smear the compound-butter all over the chicken, making sure that the chicken is evenly coated.

Pour the white wine in the bottom of the roasting pan, and place the chicken in the oven. After 10 minutes, reduce the heat to 350°F. Roast the chicken for an additional 40 to 50 minutes, until it is brown and the juices run clear if the skin is pricked—although I do not recommend pricking the chicken as it releases way too much juice. It's done when an instant-read thermometer reads 160 to 165°F.

Remove the chicken from the oven and transfer it to a carving board. Let it rest for 20 to 30 minutes before carving. Scrape the brown bits from the roasting pan with a wooden spoon or metal spatula, and skim some fat from the pan juices. Carve the chicken and place the pieces on a serving tray. Drizzle some sauce over the chicken, but reserve the majority of the sauce to serve alongside.

Honey Bear's-and-Polly's Mixed Berry Crumble

Makes 1 large or 6 to 8 individual crumbles

4 cups strawberries, stems removed, and cut in half
4 cups blueberries
2½ cups sugar, divided
2 teaspoons salt, divided
2 cups all-purpose flour
2 teaspoons baking powder
2 eggs
10 ounces (2½ sticks) butter, melted
4 tablespoons plain granola
¼ cup light brown sugar, firmly packed
Perfect French Vanilla Ice Cream, recipe follows,
    for serving

Preheat the oven to 375°F. Butter a 9 by 13-inch baking dish, or 6 to 8 ramekins.

In a large mixing bowl, combine the berries, ½ cup of the sugar, and ¼ teaspoon of the salt.

In another large mixing bowl, whisk together the remaining 2 cups of sugar, 1¾ teaspoons salt, the flour, and the baking powder. Add the two eggs and, with a fork or your hands, combine the mixture until coarse crumbs form.

Pour the fruit into the bottom of the prepared dish—or divide it evenly among the ramekins—and then top it with the crumbs. Pour the melted butter on top of the crumbs, and then the granola and brown sugar on top of the crumble. Bake until the crumble is golden brown, 30 to 35 minutes, and let it rest at least 10 minutes before serving it with Perfect French Vanilla Ice Cream.

Perfect French Vanilla Ice Cream

Makes 6 to 8 servings

2½ cups heavy cream
1½ cups whole milk
1 tablespoon plus 2½ teaspoons pure vanilla extract
8 egg yolks
1¼ cups sugar
¾ teaspoon salt

Whisk the ingredients together in a large mixing bowl to combine them but do not beat them. Place them in an ice-cream maker, and process them according to the manufacturer's instructions.

Betsy, photographed by Horst, 1961.

WHY NOT
EASTER?

ROQUEFORT GRAPES

DEVILED EGGS WITH
SMOKED SALMON

ASPARAGUS AND LEEK SOUP
WITH PERFECT SEA SCALLOPS

PERFECT ROAST LEG OF LAMB WITH
MY ALL-TIME FAVE LAMB SAUCE

MUSHY PEAS

ORANGE BOURBON POUND CAKE
WITH HOMEMADE BOURBON-PECAN
PRALINE ICE CREAM

Rule of thumb: always think of the theatre of presentation when you're planning a special day. The gorgeous and impressive roast that's the centerpiece of this menu has such style, and such sense of occasion, that it's surely elegant enough to say "Easter dinner"—yet it's easy enough to prepare if it's just another Tuesday night at home. Whether it's a holiday or not, few other dishes command the ceremony and awe that the Perfect Roast Leg of Lamb straight from the oven does. Complete crowd-pleaser—mark my words!

Here are a few important things to remember: only you know your oven so be careful on cooking times. Let the meat rest after it's cooked. I know it's tempting to carve the lamb right away, but I can't tell you how crucial this step is. I find that fifteen minutes of resting is just about the ideal time for that perfect pink—the succulent medium temperature I love for lamb. I really don't enjoy medium-rare lamb but if you do, cook it about ten to twelve minutes less and then let it rest the same fifteen minutes, just don't hold me responsible . . . and please note that if you are going for well-done, let the lamb rest more like thirty to forty minutes, as it will continue to cook even when it's out of the oven. I only love well-done lamb if it can be cut with

a spoon and is falling off the bone, so if that's your pleasure, see "Cozy and Decadent: A Winter Evening," page 200, for a slow-braised super-tender masterpiece I call, "T's Braised Lamb Shanks," but that's a completely different recipe and technique. To me, without long, slow braising, medium is just right for lamb.

As for the soup, it's another wonderful food memory. I fell in love with *flavor* at an early age in France, where I traveled often with my parents. In the 1970s, nothing there tasted like it did in America—the tomatoes, the eggs, the peaches, the asparagus—everything was so different, so vivid, so much itself. This soup is the closest thing I know to the French asparagus soup of my childhood, resplendent with what seemed exotic to me at the time: leeks, luscious chicken stock, and cream. You'll find neither cornstarch—horrors!—or flour in this soup: the scrumptious thickness comes, ever so slightly, from a sole small potato.

Even though asparagus is readily available all year long, the height of the season is early spring. Take advantage of it—you'll notice a huge difference. As a first or main course at lunch or dinner, with or without Perfect Sea Scallops, there's just no way to go wrong. If you're as hooked on this soup as I am, add poached shrimp, fresh lump crabmeat, or even sautéed chicken medallions for a light but luxurious lunch. In less than thirty minutes you'll have a completely versatile, cosmopolitan but homey, bursting-with-exquisite-flavor soup. Please don't share *how easy* it is, because your guests will think you've been simmering and prepping for days.

Roquefort Grapes

Makes 60 bite-sized hors d'oeuvres

6 ounces Roquefort cheese, crumbled
8 ounces cream cheese, at room temperature
3 tablespoons heavy cream
3 tablespoons chopped fresh chives
1 teaspoon freshly squeezed lemon juice
1¾ teaspoons salt, divided
¼ teaspoon ground black pepper
60 seedless grapes, red or green, or mixed
3 cups chopped pecans, roasted

In the bowl of an electric stand mixer fitted with the paddle attachment, combine the Roquefort cheese, cream cheese, heavy cream, chives, lemon juice, 1 teaspoon of the salt, and the ground black pepper. Turn the mixer to low speed and beat the ingredients until they are thoroughly combined, approximately 3 to 4 minutes. Turn the mixer off, remove the bowl from the stand, and add the grapes. Stir the mixture with a rubber spatula so as not to break the grapes, and scrape it onto a 9 by 13-inch baking sheet lined with parchment paper. Flatten the mixture gently with the spatula to approximately 1½-inch thickness, but again, be careful not to break the grapes. In a mixing bowl, combine the roasted pecans with the remaining ¾ teaspoon salt, and stir them well so that all of the salt is absorbed into the pecans and there is none left in the mixing bowl.

Line another 9 by 13-inch baking sheet with parchment paper and set it aside. Pour the salted pecans, and any remaining salt from the bowl, over the cheese and grape mixture, and then separate the grapes, one by one, rolling them to make sure every morsel of the cheese mixture is covered with pecans. Place the finished grapes on the second parchment-lined baking sheet, cover it with plastic wrap, and refrigerate the grapes for at least 1½ hours—but up to 3 days—before serving.

Deviled Eggs with Smoked Salmon

Makes 16 hors d'oeuvres

8 hard-boiled eggs
¼ cup Perfect Homemade Mayonnaise, page 28,
    or Hellman's
1 teaspoon Dijon mustard
1 tablespoon lemon juice
1 tablespoon chopped fresh dill
1 tablespoon chopped chives
¼ teaspoon salt
⅛ tablespoon ground black pepper
3 slices best-quality smoked salmon or Gravlax, page 40,
    1 slice diced, and the other 2 slices cut into ¼-inch-
    wide strips

Peel the hard-boiled eggs, slice them in two, and then remove the yolks from the whites. Place the yolks in a small mixing bowl and the whites side by side on a small baking sheet.

Combine the yolks with the remaining ingredients and mash them with a fork until they are smooth. Return them to the whites, divided evenly, with either a spoon, or, if you feel creative, a pastry bag fitted with a medium-size star tip.

Garnish the eggs with strips of smoked salmon, crossed, cover them with plastic wrap, and let them chill in the refrigerator for at least 1 hour or overnight.

If you've got silver stored away in a cupboard, why not just polish it up and use it? And, if you don't, call Beverly Bremer Silver Shop in Atlanta, and get some!

Asparagus and Leek Soup with Perfect Sea Scallops

Makes 10 to 12 servings

8 tablespoons (1 stick) butter
8 leeks, the white parts only, coarsely chopped
6 cups water
1 small baking potato, peeled and chopped
2½ teaspoons salt
½ teaspoon ground black pepper
½ teaspoon cracked black pepper
1 cup chicken stock
3 pounds fresh asparagus, trimmed, peeled, and coarsely chopped
1 cup heavy cream
Perfect Sea Scallops, recipe follows

Melt the butter in a medium-size heavy stockpot over medium-high heat. When the foaming has subsided, turn the heat to low, and add the leeks. Let them steep until they are soft, approximately 10 to 12 minutes. Do not let them brown.

Add the water, the potato, salt, both peppers, and the chicken stock, and turn the heat back up to medium-high. Let the mixture simmer for 15 to 20 minutes, until the potatoes are soft. Add the asparagus, and bring the soup to a boil for 10 to 12 minutes, until it has reduced by approximately one-quarter. Remove the mixture from the heat.

In a food processor fitted with a metal blade, puree the soup, in batches, until it is very smooth. Transfer the soup to a bowl, and stir in the heavy cream.

When it's time to serve, place 2 to 3 Perfect Sea Scallops in the bottom of each bowl before adding the soup.

PERFECT SEA SCALLOPS
Makes 20 to 30 scallops

3 tablespoons butter
1 tablespoon olive oil
1 pound medium sea scallops (approximately 20–30 scallops)
½ teaspoon salt
¼ teaspoon ground black pepper
1 tablespoon minced garlic
¼ cup dry vermouth
1 tablespoon lemon juice
1 tablespoon chopped fresh parsley, for garnish

In a heavy nonstick skillet over high heat, heat the butter and oil together.

Place the scallops, salt, and pepper in a medium-size mixing bowl, and toss them with the seasonings.

When the butter and oil's foaming has subsided, place the scallops in the pan and sauté them for 3 minutes, until a brown crust forms. Turn the heat down to medium-low, and turn over the scallops. Add the garlic, vermouth, and lemon juice, and sauté them for 1 more minute, and then turn off the heat. Remove the scallops with tongs, and place 2 to 3 scallops on the bottom of each soup bowl before adding the soup.

To serve the scallops on their own, place them on a serving platter, pour the remaining sauce from the pan over them, and garnish them with the parsley.

Perfect Roast Leg of Lamb with My All-Time Fave Lamb Sauce

Makes 10 to 12 servings

1 (6 ½- to 7-pound) bone-in leg of lamb
1 tablespoon plus 1 teaspoon salt
1 tablespoon coarsely ground black pepper
½ cup Easiest, Best Vinaigrette in the World, page 28
¼ cup fresh lemon juice
16 cloves garlic, peeled
½ cup fresh rosemary leaves

Preheat the oven to 400°F. Place the lamb in a large mixing bowl or roasting pan, add the salt and pepper, and toss them to combine, making sure every morsel of the salt and pepper is applied to all sides of the lamb. Place the seasoned lamb in a roasting pan. In another bowl, whisk the vinaigrette and lemon juice together.

Using a pastry brush, baste the lamb all over with the vinaigrette–lemon juice mixture. Cut 8 small slits with a pairing knife in random places in the lamb, and insert a clove of garlic in each. Process the remaining 8 cloves garlic and the rosemary together in a food processor until it is chunky but not yet pureed and pat the mixture over top of the lamb.

Place the roasting pan in the oven, and let the lamb roast for 30 minutes. Reduce the heat to 350°F, and roast the lamb for 1 more hour for medium—an internal temperature of 145 to 150°F when measured with a meat thermometer.

Remove the lamb from the roasting pan and let it rest for at least 15 minutes before carving; reserve the pan juices for the sauce below.

MY ALL-TIME FAVE LAMB SAUCE
Makes 4 cups

1 cup chopped fresh parsley
½ cup chopped fresh chives
2 tablespoons chopped fresh rosemary
4 cups diced onion
1 teaspoon minced garlic
3 cups chicken stock
1 cup red wine

1 teaspoon salt
½ teaspoon ground black pepper
2 tablespoons dry sherry
4 tablespoons (½ stick) cold butter, cut into small cubes

Once the lamb has been removed from the roasting pan, position the pan over the burners on your stove. Over low heat, add the herbs, onions, and garlic, and stir it to combine the vegetables with the pan drippings. Add 1½ cups of the chicken stock and ½ cup of the wine to deglaze the pan, scraping the bottom constantly to remove the cooked bits. Pour the mixture into a heavy saucepan with the remaining stock and wine, the salt, ground black pepper, and sherry.

Reduce the mixture over high heat until it has thickened slightly and can coat the back of a spoon, approximately 15 minutes. Strain the sauce through a fine sieve into a mixing bowl, and vigorously whisk in the cold butter. Transfer the sauce to a serving bowl, and serve it alongside the carved lamb.

Mushy Peas

Makes 10 to 12 servings

2 (16-ounce) packages frozen peas
1 (16-ounce) package frozen peas and pearl onions
3 tablespoons heavy cream
4 tablespoons (½ stick) butter, melted
½ teaspoon salt
¼ teaspoon ground black pepper

In two separate small saucepans, thaw the frozen peas, and the frozen peas and pearl onions, over low heat until they are just warm. In a food processor fitted with a metal blade, puree the thawed peas and heavy cream until they are smooth. Do not puree the peas and pearl onions.

In a mixing bowl, stir the pureed peas into the whole peas and pearl onions, and add the melted butter, salt, and pepper. Transfer the mixture to a covered baking dish, and keep it warm in a very low oven while the lamb rests.

Orange Bourbon Pound Cake

Makes 10 to 12 servings

FOR THE CAKE:
1 pound (4 sticks) butter at room temperature
2 cups sugar
1 tablespoon pure vanilla extract
1⅛ teaspoons pure almond extract
6 eggs, at room temperature
1⅛ teaspoons salt
1 teaspoon baking powder
2 cups cake flour

FOR THE GLAZE:
2 cups heavy cream
1½ cups sugar
1 tablespoon pure vanilla extract
1 tablespoon excellent-quality Bourbon
The zest of 4 large navel oranges

Preheat the oven to 325°F. Butter a 10-inch nonstick Bundt pan.

TO MAKE THE CAKE:
In the bowl of a stand mixer fitted with the paddle attachment, beat the butter on medium-high speed for about 2 minutes, until it starts to lighten in color. Add the sugar, and continue to beat until the mixture is light and fluffy, no more than 5 minutes. Turn the mixer to the lowest speed, add the vanilla and almond extracts, and then, one at a time, add 4 of the 6 eggs. Turn the mixer off, making sure not to overmix.

In a medium bowl, whisk the salt, baking powder, and flour together. Turn the mixer back on to the lowest speed. Add one-third of the flour mixture, letting it beat until it's just combined. Add another one-third of the flour mixture, and let it beat until it's just combined. Then add the rest of the flour mixture and let it beat until it's just combined. Add the remaining 2 eggs, one at a time, and beat the batter until the eggs are just combined. (I know I already said this but please be careful not to overmix this batter or your cake will be tough.)

With a rubber spatula, transfer the batter to the prepared Bundt pan and bang it on the counter three times to get rid of any excess air bubbles.

Place the Bundt pan in the oven, and bake the cake for 60 to 70 minutes, until it's golden brown and just cracked. Let the cake cool on a rack for 20 minutes, and then invert it onto a cake stand with a lip—so the glaze will not run off—and let it cool for another hour.

TO MAKE THE GLAZE:
In a large heavy saucepan over medium heat, combine the glaze ingredients and bring to a boil. Turn off the heat, and let the glaze cool for 5 minutes. Pierce the cake all over on all sides with a fork. Spoon the glaze very slowly over the cake to ensure it soaks into the pierced parts, and let it cool again. Do not refrigerate the cake; let it sit at room temperature for at least 12 hours, but preferably overnight if you can wait that long, before serving it.

Homemade Bourbon-Pecan Praline Ice Cream

Makes 1½ quarts, 10 to 12 servings

2½ cups heavy cream
1½ cups whole milk
1 tablespoon plus 2½ teaspoons pure vanilla extract
8 egg yolks
1¼ cups sugar
¾ teaspoon salt
Foolproof Bourbon-Pecan Pralines, page 52

Place the heavy cream, milk, vanilla, egg yolks, sugar, and salt in an ice-cream maker, and process according to the manufacturer's instructions. When it's finished, the ice cream will be fairly soft and will need to be frozen again for at least 4 hours, but preferably overnight. Chop the pralines and stir them into the ice cream—this will be a scrumptious mess—before refreezing the ice cream, and serving it the next day.

SPRING, GLORIOUS SPRING

PERFECT SOFT-SHELL CRABS
WITH SHIITAKE MUSHROOMS

RED FRENCH CHICKEN

ONION RICE

LUSCIOUS LEMON CURD TART
WITH CANDIED GINGER

Spring was my mother's favorite time—its flowers, its colors, its hope, its light, its rebirth. Every year she started spring, regardless of the calendar, on December 26th, banishing the garlands and bows, and filling our house in Atlanta with daffodils, crocuses, lilies of the valley, and tulips. She continued the vernal theme until early June, when she left for four months to spend the summer and early fall at our house in France. But during the winter months, if she'd scratch an informal note, send flowers, fax congratulations, or write a condolence letter, no matter the message, each missive would inevitably end with her very own communiqué of hope: "Spring is coming. Love, Caroline."

In March 1995, six weeks after my mother died, my stepfather conducted Mahler's Eighth Symphony at Carnegie Hall, the blockbuster masterpiece with more than one thousand orchestra and chorus members on stage. After the concert, there was a gala benefit at the Waldorf Astoria that my mother had been in the process of chairing for the previous two years with two New York ladies. I went alone, Robert unable to face any social situations without his beloved wife. It was a dinner dance for one thousand guests, the start of a huge capital campaign for Carnegie Hall, and was one of the most dramatically gorgeous and yet simple schemes I'd ever seen: floor-to-ceiling cherry blossoms, dogwoods, and azaleas, all dramatically lit from underneath, and varied glass vases of tulips, hyacinth, and peonies on the tables. I told one of the co-chairmen how beautiful it was, and she took a small moment to reply, her almond-shaped eyes set deliberately on me: "But what else would a proper Southern lady like in the spring?"

So, this simple, straightforward menu is my own homage to my spring-loving mother, with the things she unconditionally adored: soft-shell crabs, a classic French chicken dish that's hearty and soul-feeding yet, at the same time, easy, delicate, and complex, the simple combination of rice, butter, and onions—one of her very favorite things in the world—and a bold and fantastic lemon tart that's such a snap it very nearly makes itself. These photos were shot at the Caroline Sauls Hitz Shaw Boxwood Garden, which we excavated and restored to its original plan, and then gave in her memory in 1997 to Atlanta's Swan House, owned by the historical society for which Mom served as a trustee for more than thirty-five years, because, and I'll think you'll agree, it just seemed right to do it there.

ABOVE: *My mother, 1968.* OPPOSITE: *How's this for a recipe? Printed cotton from Quadrille for the table; dense yet super-fine Irish linen from Leontine Linens for napkins.*

Perfect Soft-Shell Crabs with Shiitake Mushrooms

Makes 8 servings, allowing 1 crab per person

8 small soft-shell crabs, defaced, and gills and aprons removed—ask your fishmonger
1 ¼ teaspoons salt, divided
1 teaspoon ground black pepper, divided
1 cup all-purpose flour
10 ounces (2½ sticks) butter, divided
2 cups shiitake mushrooms
1¼ cups golden sherry
6 tablespoons freshly squeezed lemon juice

Arrange the crabs on a baking sheet and season them on each side with ¼ teaspoon salt and ⅛ teaspoon black pepper—a total of ½ teaspoon salt and ¼ teaspoon black pepper total for the crabs.

In a medium mixing bowl, combine the flour, ½ teaspoon of the salt, and ¼ teaspoon of the black pepper.

In a large heavy skillet over high heat, melt 8 tablespoons (1 stick) of the butter. Dredge the crabs on both sides in the seasoned flour, and shake off the excess. When the foaming of the butter has subsided, add the crabs to the pan and sauté them until a light golden brown crust forms on the bottom side, approximately 2½ to 3 minutes. Turn the crabs, and add 3 more tablespoons of the butter. Let the crabs cook for another 2 to 3 minutes, then transfer them to a 9 by 13-inch baking dish or serving platter, and set them aside.

Add the remaining 9 tablespoons of butter to the skillet, and let it melt—which it should do fairly quickly as the pan will be very hot—and add the mushrooms. Add the remaining ¼ teaspoon salt and ¼ teaspoon black pepper to the pan, and sauté the mushrooms for approximately 5 minutes until they are soft. Add the sherry and lemon juice, and deglaze the pan with a metal spatula to release the brown bits sticking to the bottom of the pan. Bring the sauce to a boil for 3 to 5 minutes until it has just thickened. Turn off the heat, pour the sauce and mushrooms over the reserved crabs, and serve them immediately.

Red French Chicken

Makes 8 servings, allowing 1 thigh per person

4 pounds bone-in, skin-on, chicken thighs
2 teaspoons salt
1 teaspoon ground black pepper
1 teaspoon dried thyme
8 tablespoons (1 stick) butter, divided
2 tablespoons olive oil
6 very ripe tomatoes, skinned, seeded,
   and coarsely chopped
1 cup best-quality red wine vinegar
1 cup chicken stock
½ large red onion, cut into rings
2 tablespoons chopped fresh parsley

Preheat the oven to 350°F. In a medium mixing bowl, combine the chicken, salt, pepper, and thyme, and toss them together until the chicken is fully coated with the seasonings. In a large cast-iron skillet over medium-high heat, melt 4 tablespoons of the butter with the oil. When the foaming has subsided, add the chicken in batches, skin side down, and sear it until it's browned, about 5 minutes. Turn the chicken pieces, and sear them for an additional 5 minutes, until both sides of the chicken are brown and crisp.

Add the chopped tomatoes, and continue to sauté until the tomatoes are fairly dry, dark red, and sticky, about 10 minutes. Pour in the vinegar, and turn the heat to high. Let the chicken simmer until the liquid has almost completely evaporated, about 5 minutes. Add the chicken stock and red onion, and continue to simmer until the sauce is reduced by half, about 5 more minutes.

Transfer the chicken to a 9 by 13-inch baking dish, and pour the contents of the pan over the chicken. Cover the dish with aluminum foil and bake it in the oven for 45 minutes, until the chicken is very tender.

When the chicken's done, remove it from the oven, and use tongs to transfer the chicken from the baking dish, and into another 9 by 13-inch baking dish to serve. Pour the mushy vegetables and pan juices into a colander or sieve set over a bowl to drain the liquid.

In the new baking dish, smear the mushy vegetables over the chicken. Remove the colander or sieve from the bowl, and whisk the juices in the bowl until they are combined, and then whisk the remaining 4 tablespoons of cold butter into the sauce to give it a glossy finish. Stir in the parsley. Pour the sauce over the chicken and serve.

Onion Rice

Makes 8 to 10 servings

10 tablespoons (1 stick plus 2 tablespoons)
   butter, divided
1 large yellow or white onion, diced
4 cups long-grain or jasmine rice
2½ teaspoons salt
1¾ teaspoons freshly ground black pepper
4 cups water
4¼ cups chicken stock

Melt 8 tablespoons of the butter in a large enameled Dutch oven over medium heat. When the foaming has subsided, add the onions, and rice. Cook them until the onions and rice are translucent, 5 to 8 minutes. Add the salt, black pepper, water, and chicken stock, and turn the heat to low, cover the pot, and let the onions and rice simmer until the liquid is absorbed and the rice is tender, about 20 minutes. Stir the pot often so that the rice does not scorch. Remove the rice from the heat, and stir in the remaining 2 tablespoons butter before serving. This dish is very nearly impossible to ruin, its flavors getting better as it ages, and can be reheated and served for as many as 4 days later.

Luscious Lemon Curd Tart with Candied Ginger

Makes 8 to 10 servings

The zest of 8 lemons, finely chopped
2¼ cups plus 2 tablespoons sugar
6 tablespoons minced fresh ginger
1¾ teaspoons salt
18 tablespoons (2 sticks plus 2 tablespoons)
   cold butter, cut into cubes
8 eggs
1¼ cups fresh lemon juice
Perfect-Every-Time Pâte Brisée, page 27
Candied ginger and whipped cream for garnish

TO MAKE THE LEMON CURD:
In the bowl of a food processor fitted with the metal blade, place the lemon zest, sugar, ginger, and salt. Let the machine run until this mixture is well blended, 2 to 3 minutes.

In the bowl of an electric stand mixer fitted with the paddle attachment, cream the butter with the sugar-zest mixture on medium speed until they have lightened in color and texture, approximately 3 minutes, and then add the eggs, one at a time. Add the lemon juice, and let the mixture beat for another minute to combine.

Pour the mixture into a medium saucepan over medium-low heat, and stir it constantly with a rubber spatula until it has thickened, 25 to 30 minutes. Pour the curd into a bowl, and let it cool before covering it, and setting it in the refrigerator overnight.

TO ASSEMBLE THE TART:
Using a rubber spatula to transfer the lemon curd into the cooled prebaked shell, refrigerate the tart for at least 1 hour, and up to 3 days, before garnishing it with candied ginger and whipped cream, and serving.

In Mom's garden at the Swan House, July 2011.

THE QUINTESSENTIAL SUMMER DINNER

HEIRLOOM TOMATO AND PEACH SALAD WITH BURRATA

FALLING-OFF-THE-BONE BARBECUE CHICKEN WITH CAROLINA BARBECUE SAUCE

GRILLED SUMMER VEGETABLES

RANCH SLAW

PURPLE POTATO SALAD

SUMMER BERRY PAVLOVA WITH BOURBON WHIPPED CREAM

August in Los Angeles is *pure* magic. Simply put, it's the very best place in the world to be. No thunderstorms to dodge like on the East Coast, no crowds, train strikes, or canceled planes like in Europe. And every single day is virtually the same: eighty-two degrees, full sun, no humidity, and a blue sky that only Walt Disney could dream up. For the past twenty-plus years, on the third Wednesday night of August, I have given a dinner that varies in size, from twelve in its infancy to more than one hundred fifty now. With a table set outside, the twinkling stars above, an ever-so-soft warm breeze blowing, and the faint smell of honeysuckle in the air, I guess it's like what having dinner in heaven might be.

Just like so many things in this book—most in fact—everything on this menu, with the exception of the assembling of the pavlova, can be done ahead of time, and is, in fact, much better when you do so ahead of time. Cook the chicken a week before and reheat it! The longer the ranch slaw marinates, the better—up to three days. Same with the grilled vegetables, which can be made up to a day in advance.

As for the Peach and Tomato Salad with Burrata, I first published that recipe several years ago in *House Beautiful*, and it's a recipe I invented. It started a trend, and I now see it on catering spread after catering spread, lots of restaurant menus, and even at salad chop shops like Sweetgreen. No wonder! It's so easy, delicious, gorgeous, and popular, that I want you to enjoy it, too. The other triumph here is the homemade barbecue sauce, which is simple and splendid; you'll use it again and again on the oh-so-many things your dear family's grillmaster will inevitably overcook on the grill. Another glory of a menu like this is that virtually everything can be served room temperature—with the exception of the chicken, which you'll want slightly warm. But, even if you can't muster that, no one will die. There's just really no way to go wrong here.

Remember how God is in the details? Always add
a little slice of lemon to the water glasses on the table.

Heirloom Tomato and Peach Salad with Burrata

Makes 10 servings

2 pounds heirloom tomatoes, quartered,
    cut into eighths, and then halved
2 pounds ripe peaches, pitted, peeled, quartered,
    cut into eighths, and then halved
4 tablespoons fresh basil chiffonade
6 tablespoons olive oil
3 tablespoons balsamic vinegar
1 teaspoon salt
¾ teaspoon ground black pepper
8 ounces excellent-quality Burrata, sliced

Combine all of the ingredients, except for the Burrata, in a large mixing bowl. Toss them well. Place the salad on a serving platter, and top it with generous slices of the Burrata, before serving it immediately.

Falling-Off-the-Bone Barbecue Chicken with Carolina Barbecue Sauce

Makes 10 servings

5 pounds bone-in, skin-on chicken thighs
1 teaspoon salt
½ teaspoon ground black pepper
4 tablespoons (½ stick) butter
2 cups Carolina Barbecue Sauce, recipe follows
2½ cups chicken stock
1 large white or yellow onion, cut in half, and then thinly sliced into half-moons

Preheat the oven to 325°F. In a medium bowl, toss the chicken thighs with the salt and pepper until they are thoroughly coated. In a large heavy skillet over medium heat, melt the butter. When the foaming has subsided, sear the thighs until the skin is crisp and blackened in places.

Assemble a 9 by 13-inch baking dish with the seared thighs, 1 cup of the barbecue sauce, and the chicken stock. Place the sliced onions on the top and cover the baking dish tightly with aluminum foil. Bake the chicken for 2 hours 15 minutes. Remove it from the oven and transfer the chicken to a serving dish. Pour the remaining barbecue sauce on top of the chicken before serving.

CAROLINA BARBECUE SAUCE
1½ pounds (6 sticks) butter, melted
2½ cups apple cider vinegar
2½ cups red wine vinegar
¾ cup dry mustard
1⅞ cups Dijon mustard
2½ teaspoons celery seed
2 tablespoons salt
¾ cup minced garlic
1½ cups dark brown sugar, firmly packed
¾ cup fresh lemon juice
2 teaspoons freshly ground nutmeg

Combine all ingredients in a medium saucepan over medium heat. Stir the sauce until the brown sugar melts, approximately 5 to 7 minutes. Do not let the sauce boil.

Grilled Summer Vegetables

Makes 10 servings

3 pounds mixed vegetables, quartered—zucchini,
    yellow squash, eggplant, tomatoes, whatever you like
Essential Dill Vinaigrette, page 27

Combine the vegetables in a large mixing bowl.
Toss them with three quarters of the vinaigrette and
marinate them overnight in the refrigerator.
Reserve and refrigerate the remaining vinaigrette.

The next day, heat the grill, and remove the vegetables from the refrigerator to bring them to room
temperature. Grill the vegetables until they are fully
cooked but not too soft, and then cut them into
whatever shapes you like to serve. Toss them with the
remaining vinaigrette, and serve them slightly warm,
room temperature, or cold.

Ranch Slaw

Makes 10 to 12 servings

12 cups green cabbage, shredded,
    approximately 3 heads
½ cup fresh chives, chopped
½ teaspoon salt
¼ teaspoon freshly ground black pepper
2 tablespoons sugar
Alex's Ranch Dressing, recipe follows
1 cup chopped fresh parsley leaves

In a large mixing bowl combine the green cabbage,
chives, salt, pepper, sugar, and the ranch dressing, and
toss the slaw thoroughly to fully coat the cabbage.
Toss in the parsley. Cover the bowl with plastic wrap
and refrigerate the slaw for at least 3 hours and up
to 3 days before serving.

ALEX'S RANCH DRESSING
Makes 1¼ cups

¾ cup Perfect Homemade Mayonnaise, page 28,
    or Hellman's
¼ cup buttermilk
¼ cup white vinegar
1 teaspoon Dijon mustard
1 tablespoon minced garlic
¼ cup chopped chives
½ teaspoon salt
¼ teaspoon ground black pepper
½ teaspoon dried oregano

In a medium bowl, whisk together the mayonnaise,
buttermilk, white vinegar, Dijon mustard, garlic, chives,
salt, black pepper, and oregano until they are smooth
and well-combined. Cover the bowl and refrigerate it
for at least 4 hours and up to 4 days before serving.

Purple Potato Salad

Makes 10 to 12 servings

2 pounds purple potatoes, blanched
1 large shallot, chopped
4 green onions, chopped
3 tablespoons chopped fresh dill
¾ cup sour cream
2 tablespoons Dijon mustard
2 tablespoons Perfect Homemade Mayonnaise, page 28,
    or Hellman's
¾ teaspoon salt
¼ teaspoon ground black pepper

Boil the potatoes in a large pot of very salty water until
they are tender, about 8 to 10 minutes. Drain them in a
colander, let them cool slightly, and cut them into
quarters. Put them in a large mixing bowl, and then
add the rest of the ingredients. Using a rubber spatula,
mix the salad very well. Cover the salad and refrigerate
it for at least 4 hours or up to 3 days—as with just about
everything—the longer the better for the best flavor.

Summer Berry Pavlova with Bourbon Whipped Cream

Make 10 to 12 servings

FOR THE MERINGUE:
12 egg whites, at room temperature
4 cups superfine sugar
1 tablespoon vanilla extract
½ teaspoon cream of tartar
¾ teaspoon salt

FOR THE STEWED BERRIES:
2 cups strawberries, stemmed
2 cups raspberries
2 cups blueberries
2 cups blackberries
1½ cups granulated sugar
½ teaspoon salt
¼ cup Chambord
Bourbon Whipped Cream, page 52
Fresh mint leaves, for garnish

TO MAKE THE MERINGUE:
Preheat the oven to 250°F, and line two baking sheets with parchment paper. Draw two circles on each sheet of parchment paper using a 9-inch cake pan as a guide.

Put the egg whites, superfine sugar, vanilla extract, cream of tartar, and salt in the bowl of a stand mixer fitted with the whisk attachment, and turn the mixer to the highest speed. Let the mixer run until you can hear a palpable change in the tone of the mixer, 5 or 6 minutes. The meringue base should be thick and fluffy, and not too wet to handle without it falling back on itself. In other words, it should hold very stiff peaks.

Transfer the whipped egg white mixture to a pastry bag fitted with a large star tip. Pipe the meringue in concentric rows into the drawn circles on the parchment paper. If you're not handy with a pastry bag, just take a rubber spatula and spread the meringue on the drawn circles. The result will be more rustic but beautiful just the same.

Reduce the oven temperature to 200°F and bake the meringues for 1½ hours. Turn the oven off and leave the meringues in the oven for at least 5 hours, but preferably overnight, with the oven door closed. Do not open the oven door until the next morning. The meringues should be perfectly white and not browned in the least.

TO MAKE THE STEWED BERRIES:
Wash and dry the berries. Add all the berries, the sugar, salt, and Chambord to a large heavy saucepan over medium heat, and cook them for approximately 5 minutes, until the berries just begin to soften and the sugar dissolves. Let the mixture cool before assembling the Pavlovas.

TO MAKE THE PAVLOVA:
Assemble one of the meringues on a serving platter, and spoon one quarter of the stewed berries on top, and one quarter of the Bourbon Whipped Cream in random dollops. Place a second layer of meringue on top of the stewed berries and Bourbon Whipped Cream, and spoon another quarter of the stewed berries and whipped cream over the top. Repeat this process for the final layers. Garnish the Pavlova with fresh mint and serve.

Note: The meringues may be made up to 3 days ahead and stored in an airtight container before assembling the Pavlova.

Join us? My table for sixty at a summer dinner I gave in Los Angeles, August 2013.

A VERY
UPTOWN LUNCH
IN THE FALL

CHILLED CORN CHOWDER WITH
LUMP CRAB AND AVOCADO SALAD

SALMON-EN-CROÛTE WITH
EASIEST-EVER BÉARNAISE SAUCE

FRENCH GREEN BEANS
WITH ALMONDS

OVEN-ROASTED CHERRY TOMATOES,
PAGE 142

POIRE BELLE HÉLÈNE

PERFECT POACHED PEARS

This menu was inspired by a swell lunch I went to at my friend Annette Tapert Allen's apartment on Fifth Avenue in New York City several years ago, catered by the gold standard of New York caterers, Glorious Food. Sean Driscoll, one of the founders, and the subsequent owner once he and the original chef parted company, was a master: he understood the power of a stylish yet hearty, delicious menu coupled with elegant service, no matter the occasion. In other words, it was the whole package—it wasn't just *what* they served, it was *how* they served it. It was impossible not to notice their quality. Sean was open and cozy and unpretentious, even as he made French service the standard for seated dinners, glamourized buffets when the occasion was simpler, and always took the extra step when it came to the most minute of details. The book he did with then-partner Christopher Idone, *Glorious Food*, is as timely, stylish, and straightforward today as it was when it was printed in 1977, and not one ounce less chic.

Honestly, the only reason I love salmon now is that when I was allowed to escape the nouvelle cuisine restaurants of our family trips to France in the 1970s and 1980s, I was rewarded with the bistros and brasseries. They *always* served salmon with béarnaise sauce, *et voila!*—my love for salmon. As for the poire belle Hélène, it doesn't get more classic than this, and I am certain you'll find it exquisite, delicious, and oh so easy. I'll be right over.

ABOVE: *From left, Robert, me, Mom, Frankie Schuman, and composer William Schuman, at opening night of the Atlanta Symphony, September, 1977. When accomplished out-of-towners visited Atlanta as guest artists, my parents would give Very Uptown Lunches—in the fall, and the rest of the year, as well.*

Chilled Corn Chowder with Lump Crab and Avocado Salad

Makes 2½ quarts, enough for 10 to 12 servings

FOR THE CHILLED CORN CHOWDER:

5 pounds fresh corn on the cob, approximately 12 ears
8 tablespoons (1 stick) butter
3 pounds yellow onions, chopped
3 teaspoons salt, divided
½ teaspoon ground black pepper
7 cups whole milk
1 cup heavy cream
2 tablespoons chopped fresh cilantro, for garnish

FOR THE LUMP CRAB AND AVOCADO SALAD:

1 pound jumbo lump crab, picked for bits of shell
2 large shallots, minced
2 medium ripe avocados, pitted, peeled, and diced
1 tablespoon freshly squeezed lime juice
2 teaspoons grated lime zest
3 tablespoons Perfect Homemade Mayonnaise, page 28, or Hellman's
2 tablespoons sour cream
2 tablespoons tasteless vegetable oil
1 tablespoon apple cider vinegar
¾ teaspoon salt, divided
¼ teaspoon plus a pinch of ground black pepper

TO MAKE THE CHILLED CORN CHOWDER:

Remove the corn kernels from the cob and scrape the kernels into a mixing bowl. Run the blunt edge of your knife against the cobs to extract as much corn milk as you can into the mixing bowl. Reserve the cobs.

Melt the butter in a large stockpot over medium-high heat. When the foaming has subsided, turn the heat to medium, add the onions, and sauté them until they are translucent and soft, 20 to 25 minutes, stirring them constantly. Add the corn kernels and corn milk from the bowl, the cobs, 2 teaspoons of the salt, the ground black pepper, milk, and heavy cream, stir them together well, and bring the mixture to a boil before turning the heat down to low. Let the chowder simmer, uncovered, for an hour. Remove it from the heat, add the remaining 1 teaspoon salt, and let the chowder cool. Cover it and refrigerate it for at least 6 hours, but preferably overnight to allow the flavors to fully develop.

TO MAKE THE LUMP CRAB AND AVOCADO SALAD:

Combine all the ingredients in a medium mixing bowl and stir them carefully so as not to break the crab more than is necessary to blend the salad. Cover and refrigerate the salad for at least 4 hours, preferably overnight.

TO SERVE:

Remove the cobs from the soup, and puree the soup with an immersion blender or in a food processor in batches until it's as smooth as velvet. Stir in the chopped fresh cilantro, then ladle the chowder into individual chilled bowls. Garnish the soup with a scoop of the lump crab and avocado salad.

Salmon-en-Croûte with Easiest-Ever Béarnaise Sauce

Makes 8 servings

1 (2-pound) skinless salmon fillet, preferably cut from
    the center so it's thicker
½ teaspoon salt
¼ teaspoon freshly ground black pepper
1 (10 by 15-inch) sheet all-butter puff pastry
Mushroom Duxelles, recipe follows
Chopped fresh dill, for garnish

Preheat the oven to 375°F. Season the salmon on both
sides equally with the salt and pepper.

Place the puff pastry sheet on a heavy baking sheet, center the seasoned salmon on the puff pastry, and evenly
coat the salmon with the mushroom duxelles. Curl the
pastry up on the sides, and bake the salmon for 20 minutes, until the pastry is golden brown. Remove it from
the oven, let it rest for at least 5 minutes before transferring the salmon to a serving platter, and garnishing it
with the fresh chopped dill. The salmon may be served
up to 2 hours later at room temperature, as well.

MUSHROOM DUXELLES
Makes ½ to ¾ cup

8 tablespoons (1 stick) butter
2 pounds medium mushrooms, minced
½ teaspoon salt
¼ teaspoon ground black pepper
½ cup sherry

Melt the butter in a large heavy skillet over medium
heat. When the foaming has subsided, add the mushrooms, salt, and pepper. Reduce the heat to medium-
low, and cook the mushrooms very slowly, until all
liquid has evaporated, approximately 20 minutes. Add
the sherry, and continue to cook the mushrooms until
the sherry has evaporated, and there is no more steam
coming off of them, another 10 to 15 minutes.

EASIEST-EVER BÉARNAISE SAUCE
Makes 1 cup

¼ cup white wine
¼ cup white wine vinegar
1 tablespoon minced shallots
1½ teaspoons dried tarragon
½ teaspoon, plus a pinch of salt, divided
⅛ teaspoon freshly ground black pepper
8 tablespoons (1 stick) butter
4 egg yolks
2 tablespoons freshly squeezed lemon juice
⅛ teaspoon ground white pepper

In a large heavy saucepan over a high heat, combine
the white wine, vinegar, shallots, tarragon, pinch of salt,
and the black pepper and boil until it is thick and the
consistency of syrup, about 12 to 15 minutes. Remove
the syrup from the heat and set aside.

Melt the butter over medium heat in a heavy saucepan.
In the bowl of a food processor fitted with a metal
blade, combine the egg yolks, 1 tablespoon water,
lemon juice, remaining ½ teaspoon salt, and the white
pepper. Process them until they are thick and frothy,
approximately 2 to 3 minutes.

When the butter has melted and is fully bubbling, slowly
pour it through the tube of the food processor, drop
by drop, with the processor running. Process the sauce
until all the butter is incorporated, and a sauce emulsion forms. Remove the sauce to a warm bowl, stir in the
tarragon-shallot reduction, and serve it immediately.

French Green Beans with Almonds

Makes 8 to 10 servings

2 pounds French green beans, trimmed, and
    blanched in salted water
1 bunch long chives
4 tablespoons (½ stick) butter, melted
½ cup sliced almonds, toasted

Tie bundles of 8 to 10 green beans with a chive.
Transfer the bundles to a serving platter. Pour the melted
butter on top, sprinkle with the almonds, and serve.

Poire Belle Hélène

Makes 8 to 10 servings

Perfect Poached Pears, recipe follows
Perfect Homemade French Vanilla Ice Cream, page 146
Connie's Chocolate Sauce, page 55

Assemble the poached pears and ice cream in dessert
goblets, and drizzle them with the chocolate sauce, as
shown on page 187.

PERFECT POACHED PEARS
Makes 8 servings

1 bottle red wine or white wine, whatever color
    and variety you like
1¾ cups sugar
1 cinnamon stick
4 firm Bartlett, Anjou, or Bosc pears,
    approximately 2 pounds total
1 tablespoon freshly squeezed lemon juice
¼ teaspoon salt

In a large heavy stockpot over medium heat, simmer the
wine, sugar, and cinnamon stick together for approximately 5 minutes to let them steep. Do not boil this mixture.

Peel the pears, cut them in half lengthwise, and core
them. Add the pears to the liquid in one layer, and
gently poach them for 10 to 12 minutes, periodically
spooning the wine over them from the beginning so
that they will color evenly. When they are fork-tender
all the way through~check them after 8 minutes or
so~transfer them from the poaching liquid to a large
plate with a slotted spoon.

Let the pears cool, cover them with plastic wrap, and
refrigerate them for up to 3 days before serving. Or just
let them cool to room temperature while you finish
the sauce. Turn the heat to high and boil the poaching
liquid until it reaches a syrupy consistency, 20 to 25
minutes. Remove the sauce from the heat, and stir in
the lemon juice and salt. Place the pears on a serving
platter or individual plates, pour the sauce over them,
and serve as shown on page 205.

You can't escape the taste of the food you had as a child.
—Jacques Pépin

COZY AND DECADENT: A WINTER EVENING

BAKED ACORN SQUASH WITH
PARMESAN AND SAGE

T'S BRAISED LAMB SHANKS

BROCCOLI WITH ORANGE AND
DILL VINAIGRETTE

STONE-GROUND GRITS WITH
STILTON AND PORT

POACHED PEARS IN RED WINE WITH
HOMEMADE CARAMEL ICE CREAM

DARK CHOCOLATE GINGER SNAPS

There are seminal food memories that haunt me in the most alluring way: the succulence of the veal demi-glace with cassis on the ris de veau at Paul Bocuse's restaurant in Lyon when I was twelve; my mother's soubise, a long-cooked rice and onion dish—a recipe I've published several times—whose aroma floods my memories whenever I make it; and this exquisite, hearty braised lamb shank that was a staple of my grandmother T's dining room when I was growing up. Like every other woman on both sides of my family, T preferred playing bridge, shopping, or going to the hairdresser to cooking—and certainly did not rattle the pots daily—but she had a small, delicious repertoire, mostly of dishes that required special but simple techniques: meringues, angel food cakes, "whipped" potatoes, the very best fudge I've ever tasted, and this lamb. The only real technique required here is the browning of the lamb shanks, and, quite honestly, that's just not much of a technique at all.

Even at an unknown, and advanced age, T was still remarkably *jeune fille*: she loved clothes—preferably pale pink—and had a clanging gold charm bracelet with zillions of charms that could have easily eclipsed the one from the stage scene in *Auntie Mame*. Whenever she went out of the house she wore

ABOVE: *My father's mother, Elizabeth Crawford Hitz, whom everybody called "T," 1918.* BELOW: *T (right) with her sisters, Josephine Crawford Robinson and Hallie Crawford Kenimer, April 1965.*

big cat-eye sunglasses, pearls, and white gloves, which she kept in the glove box of her car next to the spirits of ammonia, in case she ever had a fainting spell while driving. She had a large ruby, diamond, emerald, and sapphire ring in the shape of a butterfly. She loved azaleas, hydrangeas, ranunculus, or any flower—or anything else for that matter—just so long as it was pale pink. She made it abundantly clear, when I was about eight, that a gentleman never asks a lady's age, and lied so much about her own years that, at some time in my early teens, she became younger than my father, her eldest child. She loved handsome men, always thought it just good manners to flirt, and had a quick, light touch when it came to humor.

T wondered at the reflective prisms on her chandeliers and sconces, and loved her pale turquoise linen napkins with her bold monogram, tall candles in silver sticks, ornate gold mirrors, chicken salad, cheese straws, Champagne, Brandy Alexanders, and parties. I've always thought that this snippet, on the next page, from 1932's *Atlanta Constitution*, a photo of T shopping in Buckhead—mind you, at the very height of the Great Depression—dressed in a satin cloche hat with a half-moon diamond pin, matching satin cloak, and long gloves, shows T carrying home an unsuspecting raw lamb shank from someplace like the Rhodes "Superette" for her to work her magic on.

Baked Acorn Squash
with Parmesan and Sage

Makes 6 servings

3 large acorn squashes, about 3 pounds
6 tablespoons (¾ stick) butter
6 tablespoons brown sugar
¾ cup grated Parmesan cheese
2 tablespoons chopped fresh sage leaves
½ teaspoon salt
¼ teaspoon ground black pepper

Preheat the oven to 350°F. Wash the squashes and cut them in half. Remove the seeds and place the halves, cut side up, in a 9 by 13-inch baking dish.

To each squash half add 1 tablespoon of the butter, 1 tablespoon of the brown sugar, 2 tablespoons of the Parmesan, and 1 teaspoon of the chopped sage. Sprinkle the salt and pepper over the squash halves, distributing them evenly among the halves. Cover the pan tightly with aluminum foil, and bake the squashes until they are tender if pricked with a fork, approximately 50 minutes.

Uncover the the baking dish, and continue to bake the squashes for 30 more minutes. Remove the squashes from the oven, and let it cool slightly before serving them warm.

Mrs. Alex Hitz
Enjoys Buying in Buckhead

A Brookwood Drive resident, Mrs. Alex Hitz, buys household needs in Buckhead and is a patron of Buckhead business houses for various services in home upkeep. Photo shows Mrs. Hitz with her pretty little daughter, Elizabeth, emerging from a Buckhead store.

LEFT: *T could cause a sensation even at the market, as seen with Aunt Betty in this 1932 snippet from the* Atlanta Constitution.

T's Braised Lamb Shanks

Makes 6 servings

6 lamb shanks (approximately 4 pounds)
2½ teaspoons salt, divided
1¼ teaspoons ground black pepper, divided
5 tablespoons all-purpose flour
12 tablespoons (1½ sticks) butter, divided
4 tablespoons vegetable oil
4 cups chopped onion
1 cup diced celery
1 cup diced carrots
2½ cups chicken stock, divided
2½ cups red wine, divided
1 teaspoon dried thyme
2 bay leaves
1 (28-ounce) can San Marzano tomatoes in juice

Preheat the oven to 350°F. Place the lamb shanks in a large mixing bowl, and add 2 teaspoons of the salt, and 1 teaspoon of the black pepper. Toss the shanks well to make sure every bit of the salt and pepper is absorbed into the lamb. Add the flour, and toss the lamb to coat it thoroughly.

Melt 8 tablespoons of the butter with the oil in a Dutch oven or large heavy skillet over medium-high heat. When the foaming has subsided, add the shanks. You may need to do this in batches to avoid crowding the pan. If you crowd the pan, you will steam the meat instead of browning it.

Brown, and I mean *really* brown, the shanks in the butter and oil on all sides until they are crusty, about 15 to 20 minutes. Be patient and pay attention, as this is truly the most important step of this dish. Transfer the browned shanks to a 9 by 13-inch baking dish and let them cool slightly.

Reduce the heat to low and add the remaining 4 tablespoons butter. Do not let the butter burn. The Dutch oven will be very hot. When the foaming has subsided, add the onions and sauté them for approximately 2 minutes, until they are just slightly translucent, and then add the celery and carrots. Sauté for 10 to 12 minutes more, until the vegetables are just barely soft.

Remove the cooked vegetables and all the pan juices to the baking dish or Dutch oven with the browned shanks, and then pour in 1½ cups of the chicken stock, and 1½ cups of the red wine. Add the remaining ½ teaspoon salt, ¼ teaspoon black pepper, and the thyme. Top the dish with the 2 bay leaves, spaced equally on top. Cover and bake the shanks in the preheated oven for 3 hours.

After 3 hours, add the remaining 1 cup chicken stock, 1 cup red wine, and the canned tomatoes and their juice. Cover and return to the oven for another 3 hours. After 6 hours total cooking time, remove the shanks from the oven, keep them covered, and let them rest for 25 minutes. Uncover them, discard the bay leaves, and use tongs to transfer the shanks to a serving platter. Spoon the vegetables and sauce over them, then serve.

Note: These shanks are infinitely better if they are cooked at least one day ahead, preferably two or three. Reheat them, covered, at 325°F for 45 minutes to an hour before serving.

My grandfather, here in his World War I uniform, 1917, loved this lamb so much, he and T stayed married for sixty-three years.

Broccoli with Dill and Orange Vinaigrette

Makes 8 to 10 servings

4 broccoli crowns, cut into florets
2 cups Essential Dill Vinaigrette, page 27
2 tablespoons orange zest, finely chopped
2 tablespoons freshly squeezed orange juice
½ cup plus 1 tablespoon orange marmalade

Blanch the broccoli in a large pot of salted water.
Set aside to cool in a large bowl. Whisk the remaining
ingredients together in a mixing bowl, and pour the
vinaigrette over the broccoli. I suggest warming
the vinaigrette up ever so slightly before serving it.

Stone-ground Grits with Stilton and Port

Makes 8 to 10 servings

4 cups milk, plus more if needed
1 tablespoon plus ¼ teaspoon salt
1 teaspoon cracked black pepper
¾ teaspoon freshly ground black pepper
1 tablespoon minced garlic
2 cups stone-ground grits (not instant)
¾ pound Stilton cheese, crumbled
10 tablespoons butter
¼ cup tawny port
2 teaspoons freshly squeezed lemon juice
¼ cup grated Parmesan cheese

In a large stockpot or Dutch oven over medium heat,
bring the milk, 4 cups water, salt, both peppers, and
garlic to a boil. Add the grits, reduce the heat to low,
and stir them constantly. Simmer the grits, still stirring,
until they are fully cooked through and tender, approximately 15 minutes more depending on the grits. I know
it's mentioned above but do not use instant grits.

Transfer the cooked grits to a mixing bowl and stir in
the Stilton, butter, port, lemon juice, and Parmesan
cheese. Serve the grits immediately or let them cool for
up to an hour and reheat them on low heat. When it's
time to serve, you may need to add a little additional
warm milk to the grits so they don't dry out.

Perfect Poached Pears in Red Wine with Homemade Caramel Ice Cream

Makes 6 servings

Perfect Poached Pears, page 193
2 tablespoons butter
1 pound light brown sugar
2 egg yolks
1 cup heavy cream
1 teaspoon salt
1 tablespoon plus 1 teaspoon vanilla extract
Perfect French Vanilla Ice Cream, page 146

In a medium heavy saucepan or a double boiler over low heat, combine the butter, brown sugar, egg yolks, cream, and salt, and stir them until the butter melts and the sugar dissolves. Be careful not to burn the sugar.

Remove the mixture from the heat, stir in the vanilla, and let the caramel cool completely before stirring half of it into the prepared ice cream. Refreeze the ice cream for at least 3 hours before serving. Reserve the remaining caramel to reheat, and serve it warm over the ice cream alongside the poached pears and wine sauce.

Dark Chocolate Ginger Snaps

Makes 60 small cookies

3 cups plus 2 tablespoons all-purpose flour
½ teaspoon salt
2½ teaspoons ground ginger
2 teaspoons ground cinnamon
½ teaspoon ground cloves
½ teaspoon ground nutmeg
2 tablespoons unsweetened Dutch-process cocoa powder
½ pound (2 sticks) butter, at room temperature
2 tablespoons grated fresh ginger
½ cup granulated sugar
1 cup dark brown sugar, firmly packed
1 cup unsulfured molasses
2 teaspoons baking soda
1 tablespoon warm water
14 ounces semisweet chocolate, finely chopped
Superfine sugar, for coating

Sift together the flour, salt, ground ginger, cinnamon, cloves, nutmeg, and cocoa powder. Using a stand mixer fitted with the paddle attachment, cream the butter and fresh ginger until it's light in color and fluffy, about 4 minutes. Add the white and brown sugars, then the molasses. Continue to beat until they are all thoroughly mixed.

In a small bowl, dissolve the baking soda in the warm water. Add half the flour mixture to the butter-sugar mixture, then the baking soda dissolved in warm water. Add the rest of the flour and mix thoroughly. Stir in the chocolate by hand. Turn the dough out onto a piece of plastic wrap, cover, and refrigerate for at least 2 hours or up to 1 week in advance of baking.

Preheat the oven to 350°F. Line two 9 by 13-inch baking sheets with parchment paper. Place the superfine sugar in a shallow bowl or on a plate. Using a half-ounce scoop, drop the cookies into the superfine sugar. Roll the cookies in the sugar and place them on the prepared baking sheets. Sprinkle additional superfine sugar on top.

Place the pans in the oven and bake the cookies for 3 minutes. Turn the pans and bake them an additional 3 minutes before removing them. Let the cookies cool before serving.

Probably one of the most private things in the world is an egg before it is broken.
—M. F. K. Fisher

THAT "B" WORD

CHILLED MIXED BERRY
SOUP WITH MINT

PERFECT QUICHE LORRAINE

TWICE-BAKED CHEDDAR SOUFFLÉ
WITH SHAVED TRUFFLES

GRAVLAX BENEDICT

SAUSAGE, EGG, AND
FOUR-CHEESE STRATA

BLUEBERRY SILVER-DOLLAR
CORN CAKES

LOBSTER COBB SALAD

BAKED SHALLOT CUSTARDS
WITH CAVIAR

HERB AND CHEDDAR BISCUITS

BEST-EVER BLONDIES

PECAN COFFEE CAKE

CHOCOLATE INDULGENCE CAKE
WITH MOCHA ICING

Y ou will never hear me utter the word. But there are so many splendid dishes that fall into this category that I acquiesced to the idea, and was able to write this chapter without ever actually saying it. With the exception of the poached eggs for the Gravlax Benedict, the actual cooking of the Blueberry Silver-Dollar Corn Cakes, and the second cooking of the Twice-Baked Cheddar Soufflé with Shaved Truffles, every last one of these recipes can be made ahead of time, and stay ready to be reheated whenever, for whatever. And every single dish here is a sure-fire crowd-pleaser, destined to become a back-pocket classic in your repertoire. I did not employ any uniformity for the number of people served in these recipes, as this chapter is not a specific prescription for a menu. These are merely suggested dishes, inspirations for menus you can conjure on your own by adding others of your favorite recipes, creating your own signatures, and fearlessly serving the meal that dare not speak its name.

How about this splendid color? Chilled Mixed Berry Soup with Mint, see page 210.

Chilled Mixed Berry Soup with Mint

Makes 10 to 12 servings

8 tablespoons (1 stick) butter
3 pounds yellow onions, chopped
2 teaspoons salt, divided
7 tablespoons sugar, divided
1 cup dry sherry
3 pounds fresh mixed berries, hulled if necessary, or
    flash-frozen without syrup
1 cup Chambord
1 cup milk
1 cup sour cream
Fresh mint leaves, for garnish

Melt the butter in a large stockpot over medium-high heat. When the foaming has subsided, add the chopped onions, and sauté them until they are very soft but uncolored, 20 to 25 minutes.

Add 1 teaspoon of the salt, 2 tablespoons of the sugar, and the sherry and let the onions cook another 20 minutes, until the sherry has dissolved and the onions are caramelized.

Add the berries, Chambord, the remaining 1 teaspoon salt, the remaining 5 tablespoons sugar, the milk, and sour cream. Stir the stockpot well, bring the mixture to a boil, and immediately turn off the heat.

When the soup has cooled, let it sit, covered, in the refrigerator for at least 8 hours, but preferably overnight so the flavors have the most chance to get to know each other, before pureeing it in batches in the bowl of a food processor fitted with the metal blade, or with an immersion blender until it reaches a smooth, velvet-like consistency. Serve the soup in chilled bowls, and garnish it with fresh mint.

Perfect Quiche Lorraine

Makes 8 to 10 main-course servings or 20 to 30 bite-size hors d'oeuvres

Perfect-Every-Time Pâte Brisée, page 27
1 pound cooked ham, diced
2 cups grated Gruyère cheese, firmly packed, divided
4 eggs, slightly beaten
1½ cups heavy cream
1 tablespoon Dijon mustard
¼ teaspoon nutmeg
¼ teaspoon salt
¼ teaspoon freshly ground black pepper

Preheat the oven to 350°F.

In a medium mixing bowl, thoroughly combine the ham, 1 cup of the Gruyère, the eggs, cream, mustard, nutmeg, salt, and pepper. Pour the mixture into the cooled pre-baked shell. Top the mixture with the remaining cup of Gruyère and bake it for 50 to 60 minutes, until it's golden brown. Let the quiche cool for at least 15 to 20 minutes before slicing it and serving. It can be served warm, room temperature, or cold up to 4 days after cooking—or frozen for up to a month before serving.

Twice-Baked Cheddar Soufflé with Shaved Black Truffles

Makes 6 servings

7 tablespoons butter, divided
3 tablespoons grated Parmesan cheese, divided
¾ cup milk
¼ teaspoon salt
⅛ teaspoon ground black pepper
⅛ teaspoon ground nutmeg
1 teaspoon Dijon mustard
3 tablespoons all-purpose flour
4 ounces very sharp Cheddar cheese, grated
8 large eggs, the whites only
1 teaspoon cream of tartar
Mascarpone and Parmesan Sauce, recipe follows
Fresh black truffle—as much as your budget allows,
    finely shaved

Preheat the oven to 325°F. Butter a 6-cup soufflé dish with 4 tablespoons of the butter, and 3 tablespoons of the Parmesan cheese. Set the prepared dish aside.

Heat the milk, salt, pepper, nutmeg, and Dijon mustard in a heavy saucepan over low heat. In heavy skillet over medium heat, melt the remaining 3 tablespoons butter with the flour to make a smooth roux.

When the roux has bubbled for a minute or two but not browned, pour it into the milk mixture, and whisk it vigorously to break up any lumps. Increase the heat to high, just bringing it to a boil. Turn off the heat, whisk in the grated Cheddar, and set the mixture aside.

Place the egg whites and cream of tartar in the bowl of a electric stand mixer fitted with the whisk attachment. Whisk them together on medium speed until soft peaks form, about 6 to 8 minutes. Whisk one-third of the whites into the cheese mixture, then fold in the rest, being careful not to deflate the egg whites. Gently pour the mixture into the prepared soufflé dish but do not compact it.

Assemble a bain-marie by placing the soufflé dish into a deep baking dish and pouring boiling water one-quarter of the way up the sides. Set the bain-marie in the pre-heated oven, and bake the soufflé for 18 to 20 minutes, until it has risen. Remove the soufflé from the oven, let it cool, and then invert it into an oven-to-table baking dish to get it ready to be baked again. *Note:* This recipe can be made to this point up to 3 days ahead of time. Store the cooled soufflé, covered in the refrigerator.

To rebake the soufflé, preheat the oven to 400°F. If the soufflé has been refrigerated, bring it to room temperature before rebaking it. Bake the soufflé for 8 to 10 minutes, until it's fully heated through, and has puffed up slightly again.

Remove the soufflé from the oven, place it on a warmed serving dish, pour the Mascarpone and Parmesan Sauce over it, garnish it with shaved truffles, and serve.

MASCARPONE AND PARMESAN SAUCE

16 ounces mascarpone cheese
1 cup heavy cream
1¼ cups grated Parmesan cheese
¼ teaspoon salt
⅛ teaspoon ground black pepper
1 teaspoon truffle oil

Place the mascarpone and heavy cream in a medium-sized heavy saucepan over medium-low heat, and stir them together until the mascarpone has melted and the mixture is smooth. Stir in the Parmesan cheese, salt, and pepper. When the cheese has fully melted, remove the saucepan from the heat and stir in the truffle oil. Place the mixture in the bowl of a food processor fitted with the metal blade, and process the sauce until it's completely smooth before serving it warm over the soufflé.

In the 1970s, the Roux brothers popularized twice-baked soufflés at Le Gavroche. These days, all the posh dining spots in London have one—but this one, inspired by Scott's of Mayfair—is the best.

Gravlax Benedict

Makes 4 to 6 servings

4 whole grain English muffins, split, buttered,
    and toasted
8 slices Harry's Gravlax, page 40 or best-quality
    smoked salmon
8 poached eggs
8 tablespoons Dill Hollandaise Sauce, recipe follows
Chopped fresh dill, for garnish

Assemble the toasted muffins on a warmed serving platter. Place 1 slice of Gravlax or smoked salmon on each
muffin, then top the salmon with a poached egg. Spoon
at least 1 tablespoon of sauce over each egg, garnish
them with fresh dill and serve them immediately.

DILL HOLLANDAISE SAUCE
Makes 1 cup

4 egg yolks
½ teaspoon salt
1 pinch freshly ground white pepper
8 tablespoons (1 stick) salted butter, melted
2 tablespoons fresh lemon juice
2 tablespoons chopped fresh dill

Set a double boiler over medium heat. In a medium
mixing bowl, whisk the egg yolks, 1 tablespoon water,
salt, and pepper until thick and frothy. If you're not
inspired to whisk by hand, this step may be done in an
electric stand mixer fitted with the whisk attachment,
or in a food processor fitted with the metal blade.

Pour the frothy eggs into the warmed double boiler
and reduce the heat to low. Immediately start adding
droplets of the melted butter to the egg yolk mixture
slowly but in a steady stream, whisking it constantly
over very low heat until an emulsion forms. Do not
add the butter too quickly or all at once, and make

sure the heat is low, or you will have scrambled eggs,
not hollandaise sauce. If you're not inspired to do this
by hand—and, for the record, I rarely am—heat the butter until it's bubbling, and add it in a steady stream of
droplets to the mixture in the stand mixer or through
the sleeve of a food processor while either is running.
When the butter is fully incorporated, an emulsion
will form. Remove the sauce to a serving bowl, stir in
the chopped fresh dill and serve.

Note: This recipe will be more than enough for the
Benedict, but it will surely disappear. Let any left over
sauce cool completely, then cover and refrigerate it.
Later, it will have the consistency of butter. I love cold
hollandaise sauce the next day on my morning toast,
instead of butter and jam, if it lasts that long.

*Any breakfast or 'B' word is a decadent,
spoiling treat when served on a tray, in bed.*

Sausage, Egg, and Four-Cheese Strata

Makes 16 to 20 servings

1 pound bulk pork sausage, browned and drained
2 medium onions, diced
24 eggs, slightly beaten
8 ounces Gruyère cheese, shredded
8 ounces blue cheese, crumbled
8 ounces sharp Cheddar cheese, shredded, divided
2 tablespoons grated Parmesan cheese
1½ teaspoons salt
1 teaspoon ground black pepper
¾ teaspoon ground nutmeg
1 cup fresh breadcrumbs, buttered and tossed with
    2 tablespoons of melted butter
Sour cream, for garnish
Chopped chives, for garnish

Preheat the oven to 350°F. Butter a 9 by 13-inch baking pan.

In a large mixing bowl, using a rubber spatula, combine the sausage, onions, eggs, Gruyère, blue cheese, half of the Cheddar, the Parmesan, salt, pepper, and nutmeg. Pour the mixture into the prepared baking pan, and then add the remaining Cheddar cheese, and then the breadcrumbs on top.

Bake the strata for 45 to 50 minutes, until it's just set. Let the strata cool for at least 15 minutes before serving it, but like so many of the recipes, in this book, this dish is much better when it's made at least the day beforehand and reheated, covered, for about 20 to 25 minutes at 325°F.

Blueberry Silver-Dollar Corn Cakes

Makes 12 to 14 silver-dollar-size pancakes

½ cup yellow cornmeal
1½ cups all-purpose flour
¼ cup sugar
1½ teaspoons baking powder—make sure it's new or risk the cakes not rising!
1½ teaspoons salt
2½ cups buttermilk
3 large eggs
4 tablespoons (½ stick) melted butter
1½ cups blueberries, plus additional berries for serving
6–8 tablespoons clarified butter, for the skillet
Maple syrup, for serving

In a large mixing bowl, whisk together all the ingredients except the clarified butter until they are just combined. Do not overmix the batter or the cakes will be tough. Refrigerate the batter for 30 minutes before cooking.

Heat some clarified butter in a large heavy skillet over medium heat. When it is heated through, but just before it's bubbling, add small scoops of batter in batches. Cook the cakes until they are golden brown and bubbles show through, before flipping them to finish the other side. I like them so much better when they are undercooked, but you choose.

In 1977, President Carter appointed my stepfather Robert to the National Council on the Arts, a post he kept throughout several administrations. We visited Washington often, and the first time I ever had Blueberry Corn Cakes was at The White House. Grits in pancakes? Why not?

To our good friends Caroline & Robert Shaw —
Jimmy Carter 3-80

Lobster Cobb Salad

Makes 10 to 12 servings

2 heads Romaine lettuce, large outer leaves discarded,
   cut into 2-inch strips
3 ripe avocados, halved, peeled, pitted, and cut
   into ½-inch cubes
2 pounds cooked lobster meat, seasoned with
   ½ teaspoon salt and ¼ teaspoon freshly ground
   black pepper, sautéed in 4 tablespoons butter and 2
   tablespoons vermouth, and cooled
3 large ripe tomatoes, halved, seeded, and chopped
   into ¼-inch pieces
1 cup crumbled blue cheese
8 thick slices bacon, cooked crisp and chopped
   into ¼-inch pieces
½ teaspoon salt
½ teaspoon freshly ground black pepper
The Easiest, Best Vinaigrette in the World, page 28

Combine all the ingredients in a large serving bowl.
I always layer the ingredients separately as shown at left,
with the lettuce on the bottom and the rest forming
a geometric pie-shaped pattern, as it's so much more of
an impressive presentation that way. When you are
ready to serve, add the dressing, and toss the salad at
least forty times so that it fully combines.

The very best of all chopped salads ever was called the "Nancy Reagan Salad" at a posh Los Angeles hotel. Left to right:
David Jones, Nancy, Frank Bowling, and me in Connie Wald's screening room in Beverly Hills, August 2005.

Baked Shallot Custards with Caviar

Makes 8 individual custards

10 tablespoons butter, divided
¼ cup minced shallots
16 eggs
½ cup heavy cream
10 tablespoons sour cream, divided
2 green onions, white and green parts, chopped
¾ teaspoon salt
½ teaspoons ground black pepper
4 ounces caviar—the best you can afford!
4 teaspoons lemon juice
The zest of 1 lemon, grated, and finely chopped

Preheat the oven to 325°F. Melt 8 tablespoons (1 stick) of the butter in a medium heavy skillet over medium-low heat. When the foaming has subsided, add the shallots, and sauté them for 5 to 6 minutes, until they are translucent. Remove them from the heat, and let them cool slightly.

In a large mixing bowl, combine the eggs, heavy cream, 2 tablespoons of the sour cream, the green onions, salt, pepper, and the sautéed shallots. Whisk the mixture together until it's just combined, but do not overmix, as you do not want to incorporate too much air in the mixture.

Melt the remaining 2 tablespoons butter and brush 8 (1-cup) ramekins with the melted butter. Place the ramekins in a large baking pan, and pour the egg mixture into the prepared ramekins. Set the baking dish in the oven, and assemble a bain-marie by carefully adding hot water to the baking pan one-quarter of the way up the sides of the ramekins. Let the custards bake for 25 minutes until they are just set but have not colored. Remove them from the oven, and let them cool for at least 10 minutes before serving.

To serve the custards, place each ramekin on an individual serving plate. Top each ramekin with 1 tablespoon of the remaining sour cream, 1 tablespoon caviar, ½ teaspoon of the lemon juice, and a sprinkle of lemon zest.

I never think of caviar without being reminded of New York City's very best hostess ever, Nan Kempner, who served more caviar, more often, than anybody I have ever known.

Herb and Cheddar Biscuits

Makes fifty 1½-inch biscuits

9 ounces (2 sticks plus 2 tablespoons) butter, divided
3 cups self-rising flour
2¼ teaspoons salt
1 tablespoon plus 1 teaspoon sugar
1 teaspoon dried oregano
1 teaspoon dried dill
½ teaspoon ground black pepper
1 cup small-cubed Cheddar cheese, firmly packed
2 tablespoons grated Parmesan cheese
2 teaspoons minced garlic
½ cup plus 2 tablespoons whole buttermilk
½ cup plus 2 tablespoons whole milk

Preheat the oven to 425°F. Line a large baking sheet with parchment paper.

Cut 12 tablespoons (1½ sticks) of the butter into small cubes and place them in the freezer for at least 10 minutes.

In a large mixing bowl, combine the flour, salt, sugar, oregano, dill, and ground black pepper, and whisk them together. Add the Cheddar and Parmesan cheeses, and the garlic, and mix them well.

Add the cold butter, and incorporate it into the flour by breaking up the cubes with your hands. Continue working the butter and flour together until coarse crumbs form. Pour in the buttermilk and milk, and gently stir the mixture with a rubber spatula until a very sticky dough forms. Cover the bowl with plastic wrap, and set it in the refrigerator for 30 minutes.

Melt the remaining 6 tablespoons (¾ stick) of butter. Remove the dough from the refrigerator, place it on a floured board, and knead it only a couple of times—do not knead it more than this or the biscuits will be tough and not delicate. Press the dough to a ¼-inch thickness using your hands and cut it with a 1½-inch biscuit cutter.

Line the biscuits on the prepared pan so that they are touching—this will help them rise when they are baked. Brush them with half of the melted butter, before putting them in the oven for 7 minutes. After 7 minutes, turn them, and cook them for another 3 to 4 minutes, until they are golden brown. Remove them from the oven, and brush them with the remaining melted butter before setting them on a counter or rack to let them cool.

Best-Ever Blondies

Makes about 16 to 18 (2-inch)-round blondies, or
50 to 60 small square blondies—how many that serves
is up to you; I always want about 600 of them.

1½ cups all-purpose flour
1 teaspoon baking powder
1 teaspoon salt
2 cups firmly packed light brown sugar
½ pound (2 sticks) butter, melted
1 tablespoon vanilla extract
2 large eggs
1 cup chopped pecans, toasted after chopping
½ cup semisweet chocolate chips
½ cup white chocolate chips

Preheat the oven to 350°F. Butter a 9 x 13-inch
baking pan.

In a large mixing bowl, whisk together the flour,
baking powder, and salt. In another mixing bowl, stir
together the sugar and butter, and then stir in the
vanilla. Stir the eggs into the sugar mixture, one at a
time. Add the sugar-egg mixture to the flour mixture,
and mix it to combine, then stir in the pecans and the
semisweet and white chocolate chips. Do not overmix.

Transfer the mixture to the prepared pan, and bake
it for 18 to 20 minutes, until the blondies are just set.
Like every other cookie and brownie under the sun,
the more underbaked they are but still set, the better
they are. Let the blondies cool to room temperature.
Cut them into squares—or, if you want to get fancy,
use a cookie cutter to make them into rounds as
shown opposite.

Pecan Coffee Cake

Makes 20 servings

FOR THE PECAN CRUMB:
2 cups whole pecans
1¾ cups light brown sugar, firmly packed
1½ teaspoons cinnamon
½ teaspoon nutmeg
1 teaspoon salt
½ pound (2 sticks) butter, melted

FOR THE CAKE:
1½ cups cake flour
1½ cups all-purpose flour
1½ teaspoons salt
1½ teaspoons baking powder
1¼ teaspoons baking soda
1½ cups sugar
10 ounces (2½ sticks) butter, melted
4 eggs
1 tablespoon plus 1 teaspoon pure vanilla extract
½ teaspoon almond extract
1½ cups sour cream, at room temperature
¾ cup buttermilk
Confectioners' sugar, for garnish

Preheat the oven to 350°F. Butter a 9 by 13-inch baking dish.

TO MAKE THE CRUMB TOPPING:
To the bowl of a food processor fitted with a metal blade, add the crumb ingredients and process them until they are just combined. Be careful, as tempting as it is, not to overprocess them. The topping should be coarsely chopped, not smooth.

TO MAKE THE CAKE:
In a large mixing bowl, whisk together the cake flour, salt, all-purpose flour, baking powder, baking soda, and sugar. Add the melted butter, eggs, vanilla and almond extracts, sour cream, and buttermilk, and blend them with a rubber spatula or whisk until they are just smooth. Do not overmix.

Pour half of the cake batter into the prepared baking dish and smooth it with a spatula. Add half of the pecan crumb mixture. Pour the rest of the cake batter into the baking dish, and then the rest of the crumb mixture on top. Bake the cake for 40 to 50 minutes, until a toothpick inserted in the center comes out clean. Let the coffee cake cool for at least 25 minutes before sifting confectioners' sugar on the top and serving.

Chocolate Indulgence Cake with Mocha Icing

Makes 12 servings

4 ounces unsweetened chocolate, coarsely chopped
10 tablespoons (1 stick plus 2 tablespoons) butter
1 cup very strong brewed coffee
2 eggs
1 egg yolk
2½ cups granulated sugar
1 tablespoon pure vanilla extract
½ cup sour cream
1¼ teaspoons baking soda
2 cups cake flour, plus more for the pan
1 teaspoon baking powder
¾ teaspoon salt
Mocha Icing, recipe follows

Preheat the oven to 325°F. Melt the chocolate with the butter and coffee in a heavy saucepan or double boiler. Allow the mixture to cool slightly.

In the bowl of a stand mixer fitted with the whisk attachment, beat the eggs and the egg yolk for 5 minutes on high speed, until they expand approximately four times in volume. Be patient. Gradually add the sugar and vanilla, and continue to beat for 4 to 5 more minutes at the same speed.

In a small mixing bowl, combine the sour cream and baking soda, and fold them into the egg mixture. Then fold in the melted chocolate mixture.

Sift the flour, baking powder, and salt together in a medium mixing bowl, and fold it into the egg-chocolate mixture.

Butter and flour a 10-inch tube or Bundt pan and pour the batter into pan. Bake the cake until a toothpick inserted in the center comes out clean, about 30 minutes. Let the cake cool for 20 minutes before inverting it onto a serving platter. Let the cake cool completely before icing it.

MOCHA ICING
Makes enough for one cake, if you don't eat it all first

8 tablespoons (1 stick) butter
1 cup granulated sugar
¼ cup half-and-half
2 teaspoons espresso powder
2 teaspoons pure vanilla extract
¾ teaspoon salt
2 cups confectioners' sugar, sifted

Melt the butter in a medium-sized heavy saucepan over medium heat. When the butter has melted, add the granulated sugar, half-and-half, and espresso powder. Stir the saucepan to combine them thoroughly. Bring the mixture to a boil, stirring it constantly. Remove it from the heat, add the vanilla and salt, and let it cool to room temperature.

Once it's cooled, pour the mixture into the bowl of an electric stand mixer fitted with the paddle attachment. Turn the mixer on medium speed, and gradually add the confectioners' sugar until the icing is a spreadable consistency. Do not refrigerate the icing. Ice the cooled cake, and serve.

THE ART OF THE GUEST

- Whenever you're invited, whether you can attend or not, say thank you.

- Respond to your invitations in a very timely manner, say, within four days of receiving them. Never make your host chase you for a response.

- When you leave, and after you've attended, say thank you. And then write a thank-you note.

- Always send a little present—some flowers, a case of wine, or a book. I usually send something beforehand or afterwards, as I find it causes the host great trouble to have to fiddle with a gift as guests are arriving, but that is far better than doing nothing.

- Remember: accepting an invitation means you plan to return the favor.

- Never use your cell phone—no excuses. Doing so shows you think you are more important than everyone else, and, sorry to break it to you, but that's just not true. We all had children, parents, pets, news, and emergencies before such phones and things mostly worked out just fine. Succumbing to their bells, lights, and chimes is merely feeding a dangerous, mounting, and paralyzing addiction, and, let's face it, those really just aren't that much fun at parties.

- Always bring your best energy, humor, and charm—no great party starts off with you complaining about your troubles. Everyone has those, and everyone can stay home to think about them. Go out and enjoy, take yourself out of yourself, if only for a brief time—how bad can it be?

- Never make your special needs someone else's problem—much less someone who has extended the generous gesture to invite you. In other words, do not specify your food allergies or dietary restrictions, even if asked, unless somehow you believe this to be your last meal on Earth. As with my own food allergies, these are my problem, not my host's.

- If you're at a seated dinner, at the turn of the courses, always turn to the guests, on whichever side, that you have not engaged during the previous course. Do not ignore either neighbor, even if you're engrossed in conversation. Be inclusive, not cliquish.

- Never, ever, get up from the table until the lunch or dinner is over.

- Always mingle and meet everyone you do not know. But, no matter what, do not look over the shoulder of the person you're stuck with to find someone better. Not everyone will remember what you've said, but they will remember exactly how you made them feel.

- Arrive no more than fifteen minutes after the invitation's time—and do not overstay your welcome. When it's over, it's over; don't linger pointlessly. There will be another occasion if you've acted appropriately.

- If you have accepted an invitation, never, ever, cancel after noon on the day of the party unless you have died. If you're sick, you'll have been sick by noon.

- In case you missed it above, *ALWAYS* write a thank-you note.

INDEX

ACKNOWLEDGMENTS

What is there to say but thank you? There is no way for me to verbalize my gratitude to so many people from so many different facets of my life who have specifically helped me in the writing of this book or whose support in general has enabled me to write it, so I humbly list their names in alphabetical order.

Darlene Adams, Savannah Adderley, Bruce Addison & Michael Foster, Annette & Joe Allen, Keith Arnette, Richelle Bagabaldo, Kevin Bagnold, Iain Bagwell, Natasha Bain, Nikki of Beverly Hills, Justine Bloomingdale, Polly Bloomingdale, Cynthia Boardman, Barry Braynen, Chesie Breen, Beverly Bremer Silver Shop, Nick Brock Antiques, Caroline Brown, Katherine Bryan, Doris Brynner, Victoria Brynner & Gino Sullivan, Bernadette Bunch, Nina Campbell, Daniel Cappello, Dexter Carr, Marco Carranza, Nancy Carithers, Doug Cecil, Alejandra Cicognani, Laura Church, Amy Fine Collins, David Patrick Columbia, Emily & Rodney Cook, Nathan Cooper, Larry Couzens, Torie Cox, Carl Cristiano, Sal Cristiano, Grega & Leo Daly, Brooke & Blake Davenport, Barbara Davis, Barrett Davis, Mitchell Davis, Peggy Davis, Kelly Day, Jackie & Jean-Charles de Ravenel, Drew Dinwiddie, Sara Dodd, Pierre Durand, Fontaine Draper, Betty & Bob Edge, George Farias, David Farrington, Christian Favalli, Alberto Filho, Lisa Fine, Pamela Gross Finkelstein, John Fondas & John Knott, Peggy Foreman, Nola Frink, Ormand Gibson, Sandy Golinkin, David Goldstein, Susan Gutfreund, Kasey Graham, Louise Grunwald, David Hall, Denise Hale, Theresa Hamilton, Ann & Pegram Harrison, Mary Hayley & Selim Zilkha, Brooke Hayward, Herend USA, Susan Fales-Hill, Jane Scott Hodges, Emily Hope, Marin Hopper, Nicolette Horn, Jane & Michael Horvitz, Barry Hutner, Lisa Jackson, Jono Jarrett, Liz Johnson, Guyto Joseph, Desmond Kelly, Heather Koehle, Gamini Kokowalage, The Staff of KCNY, Lynn Booth Kresa, Ristorante La Grotta, Jean-Christophe Laizeau, Richard Keith Langham, Kelly Lassiter, Leontine Linens, Jean-Paul Le Fevre, Valerie Levin, James Lewis, Rich Liblang, Amanda Lindroth, Leontine Linens, Carol and Earle Mack, Edwin Mallari, Jane Marsden Antiques, Gregory Martin, Boaz Mazor, Gail McIntosh, Amanda McLester, Alvin McRoyal, Mark Miller, Ginny & Guy Milner, Natasha Mobley, Gail Marcus Monaghan, Parc Monceau Antiques, Charlotte Moss, Margaret & Gary Motley, Christy Murray, Stephen Newbold, Sacha Newley, Shaun Newton, Ann-Marie Nieves, Ellen Niven, Kelly Nixon, Vanessa Noel, Edwin Orihuela, David Paulstich, Victoria Pearson, Peggy Peele, Jo Phelps, Kay Pick, Craig Pogdon, Quadrille Fabrics, Denisko Rahming, Lesley Rahming, Darren Ramirez, Isabel Rattazi, Suzanne Rheinstein, Rosie Roker, Danielle Rollins, Paul Romano, Chun Rosenkranz, Sarah Rousselot, Angela Russell, Christopher Santacroce, Adrian Sassoon & Edmund Burke, Frances Schultz, Monique & Ferdinand Seefried, Margot Shaw, Janice Shay, David Shulte, Primitiva Sicat, Janette Smith, Mary Louise Smith, Merle Smith, Todd Sowers, Georgia & Ron Spogli, Wendy Stark, Reuben Stuart, Jeremiah Tower, Sheamus Porter Trott, Kathryn Trussell, Doug Turshen, Steve Turner, Dot Vick, Lucy Vilchez, Stellene Volandes, Shelley Wanger, William Wayne and Company, Ruth & Hutton Wilkinson, Elizabeth Williams and Rolls Royce America, Sophie & Freddie Windsor, Kirk Whitfield, Ann & Mathew Wolf, Mimi & Gerry Woodruff, Dot Vick, William Yeoward Crystal, Lisa Zwanziger, Bettina Zilkha, Nadia Zilkha.

This is some incredible team—my dear friends and "food family" from Soiree Catering and Events in Atlanta and Mary Boyle Hataway, in green, to whom this book is co-dedicated.

PHOTO CREDITS

Front endpapers (opposite page 1): Photo by Courtney Price; page 75: Courtesy of Connie Wald; page 81: Photo by Horst; page 91: Photo by Peter Bacanovic; page 94: Courtesy of Nadia Zilkha; pages 115 and 121: Photo by Patrick McMullan; page 130: Photo by Dean King; pages 140 and 146: Courtesy of Betsy Bloomingdale; pages 148 and 151: Photo by Amy Graves; page 212: Courtesy of Scott's of Mayfair; page 215: Photo by Deborah Whitlaw-Llewellyn; page 221: Photo by Andrew Wald; page 222: Photo by Francesco Scavullo, Courtesy of Getty Images; page 232: Photo by Lisa Romerin, Courtesy of Otto Images

First published in the United States of America in 2019 by
Rizzoli International Publications, Inc.
300 Park Avenue South
New York, NY 10010
www.rizzoliusa.com

Copyright © 2019 Alex Hitz
www.alexhitz.com
Photography: Iain Bagwell
www.iainbagwell.com

Publisher: Charles Miers
Editor: Jono Jarrett
Design: Doug Turshen with Steve Turner
Production Manager: Colin Hough-Trapp
Managing Editor: Lynn Scrabis

Printed in China

2019 2020 2021 2022 / 10 9 8 7 6 5 4 3 2 1

ISBN: 978-0-8478-6355-6
Library of Congress Control Number: 2019931790

Visit us online:
Facebook.com/RizzoliNewYork
Twitter: @Rizzoli_Books
Instagram.com/RizzoliBooks
Pinterest.com/RizzoliBooks
Youtube.com/user/RizzoliNY
Issuu.com/Rizzoli